Vegetarian and Vegan Diets

ISSUES

Volume 140

Editors

Lisa Firth and Cobi Smith

Independence

Educational Publishers
Cambridge

First published by Independence
PO Box 295
Cambridge CB1 3XP
England

British Library Cataloguing in Publication Data
Vegetarian and vegan diets. - [Issues ; 140]
1. Vegetarianism 2. Veganism 3. Animal welfare - Moral and
ethical aspects
I. Firth, Lisa II. Smith, Cobi
179.3

ISBN-13: 9781861684066

Printed in Great Britain
MWL Print Group Ltd

Cover
The illustration on the front cover is by
Don Hatcher.

CONTENTS

Introduction

Vegetarian and Vegan Diets is the one hundred and fortieth volume in the **Issues** series. The aim of this series is to offer up-to-date information about important issues in our world.

Vegetarian and Vegan Diets looks at vegetarians and vegans, and at the issue of animal welfare.

The information comes from a wide variety of sources and includes:
Government reports and statistics
Newspaper reports and features
Magazine articles and surveys
Website material
Literature from lobby groups
and charitable organisations.

It is hoped that, as you read about the many aspects of the issues explored in this book, you will critically evaluate the information presented. It is important that you decide whether you are being presented with facts or opinions. Does the writer give a biased or an unbiased report? If an opinion is being expressed, do you agree with the writer?

Vegetarian and Vegan Diets offers a useful starting-point for those who need convenient access to information about the many issues involved. However, it is only a starting-point. Following each article is a URL to the relevant organisation's website, which you may wish to visit for further information.

* * * * *

Vegetarianism

Why be a vegetarian? We look at the cases for and against

What exactly is a vegetarian?

Vegetarians do not eat meat, poultry, game or fish, and also avoid slaughterhouse by-products such as gelatine, rennet and animal fats – so anyone who says, 'I'm a vegetarian but I eat chicken' is deluding themselves. Most vegetarians, however, eat dairy products and free-range eggs. In the last ten years, the number of vegetarians in the UK has more than doubled; there are currently about four million vegetarians in the UK – 7% of the adult population and 12% of young people.

Why stop eating meat?

There are lots of reasons – some choose this diet in order to reduce animal suffering, but (if done properly) it also improves personal health (see below) and safeguards the environment.

Improve your health

There was a time when vegetarians were regarded as a weird sect of pale, unhealthy types. Luckily, we've come on a bit since then and both awareness and attitudes have changed. Medical research has shown that on average, a lifelong vegetarian visits the hospital 22% less often than an average meat-eater, saving the National Health Service an estimated £45,722. Vegetarians generally suffer less heart disease, hypertension, obesity, diabetes, various cancers, diverticular disease, bowel disorders, gallstones, kidney stones, and osteoporosis (Dwyer, 1988). Vegetarian diets have also been used in the treatment of various illnesses, including rheumatoid arthritis and nephrotic syndrome.

Of course, you aren't automatically healthier just because you're veggie – these findings are based on a healthy balanced vegetarian diet. A high consumption of fresh fruit and vegetables is a benefit of balanced vegetarian diets and research has demonstrated the importance of protective antioxidant nutrients in the diet found in fresh fruit and vegetables. These antioxidant nutrients include the beta-carotene form of vitamin A, C and E. Many researchers now believe that these nutrients play a major role in reducing the risk of chronic diseases such as heart disease and cancer.

So how do I make sure my diet is balanced?

One of the easiest things to miss out on when you switch to vegetarianism is protein. There are plenty of protein-rich foods, forming four groups:

⇨ Grains – cereals, rice, pasta and bread
⇨ Pulses – chickpeas, lentils, peas and beans
⇨ Nuts and seeds – peanuts, almonds, sunflower seeds etc.
⇨ Dairy products – cheese, yoghurt, milk (and eggs)

Many nutritionists recommend that you combine foods from two groups every meal. That's not as complicated as it sounds – you'd probably have more than one of them anyway (e.g. beans on toast – beans are pulses, grains in the bread or breakfast cereal – cereal provides grains, milk is a dairy product).

What about iron?

'Every vitamin, mineral and nutrient your body needs is available in abundance on a balanced veggie diet,' says Kate Fowler, from the vegetarian campaign group, Viva.

The British Medical Association agrees. It says:

⇨ Vegetarians are no more likely to suffer from anaemia (iron deficiency) than meat eaters;
⇨ A vegetarian diet meets all the nutritional needs of adolescents;
⇨ Vegetarians have lower rates of obesity, coronary heart disease, high blood pressure, large bowel disorders, cancers and gallstones;
⇨ Vegetarians often live longer and suffer less from chronic diseases

Is it really for me?

As well as the health benefits, you may find you have extra energy, fewer illnesses, clearer skin and a clearer conscience. It's not a one-way street; you can always go back to eating meat if you aren't happy. At best you'll have started a new way of eating that'll keep you healthier for life, at worst you'll have had a go at being a veggie and found it wasn't for you.

⇨ The above information is reprinted with kind permission from TheSite.org. Visit www.thesite.org for more information.

© TheSite.org

☐ Healthier heart ☐ Less chance of cancer ☐ Breathe easier
☐ Unclogged arteries ☐ Lose the spare tyre ☐ Less chance of diabetes
☐ Cleaner bowels ☐ Avoid hypertension ☐ Avoid kidney stones

Vegetarian and vegan diets

Information from the British Nutrition Foundation

Vegetarian diets have been around for hundreds of years, but the practice has only been adopted more widely in the last 50 years. It is estimated that in the UK, between 3 and 7% of the population are vegetarian and women are more likely to be vegetarian than men. There are many interpretations of a 'vegetarian' diet, ranging from avoiding red meat most of the time through to a strict vegan diet, where all foods of animal origin are excluded.

In an omnivorous (meat-containing) diet, animal-derived foods like meat, fish, eggs and dairy products normally provide substantial amounts of food energy, protein, calcium, iron, zinc, vitamins A, D and B12. Nutritional status is at risk when appropriate substitutions are not made for any group of foods that is omitted from the diet, for whatever reason. A well-planned and varied vegetarian diet will provide adequate energy and sufficient amounts of these nutrients but problems arise if those foods excluded are not replaced by suitable alternatives in terms of the nutrients they supply. The key to a healthy, balanced vegetarian diet (as with an omnivorous diet) is an

BRITISH Nutrition FOUNDATION

understanding of the food groups that underpin a healthy diet, i.e. which foods provide which nutrients, and forward planning of meals.

Types of vegetarian diets

People follow a vegetarian diet for a variety of personal, philosophical, ecological and economical reasons. Variations in strictness of vegetarianism are largely dependent on the person's beliefs and reasons for adopting vegetarianism. This may be for a variety of personal, philosophical, ecological and economical reasons. Some understanding of these reasons is important when considering nutritional status and also when preparing meals for vegetarians, as it may be necessary to use entirely separate utensils to prepare acceptable vegetarian dishes.

All types of diets, omnivorous and vegetarian alike, have potential health risks, as well as associated benefits

---

'Semi' or 'demi' vegetatarian
Exclusion of red meat or all meat, but fish and other animal products are still consumed; some people also include poultry
Pesco-vegetarian
Exclusion of all red meat and poultry, but fish and other animal products are still consumed
Lacto-ovo-vegetarian
Exclusion of all meat, fish, poultry; milk, milk products and eggs are still consumed. Most UK vegetarians

follow a lacto-ovo-vegetarian diet
Lacto-vegetarian
Exclusion of all meat, fish and poultry and eggs; milk and milk products are still consumed
Vegan
Exclusion of all foods of animal origin; diets comprise grains, vegetables, vegetable oils, cereals, pulses such as beans and lentils, nuts, fruit and seeds. Non-food animal products, such as leather, may also be avoided.
Fruitarian
Exclusion of all foods of animal origin as well as pulses and cereals. Diets mainly comprise raw and dried fruits, nuts, honey and olive oil. People following this type of eating pattern are at great risk of nutritional deficiency; their diets require vitamin and mineral supplementation.
Macrobiotic – sometimes referred to as Zen Macrobiotic diet
The diet progresses through a series of levels, gradually eliminating all animal produce, fruit and vegetables and, at the highest level, leading to a restricted diet of cereal (brown rice) only. Fluids may also be severely restricted. Children are particularly at risk of nutritional deficiency and studies have shown that growth patterns are disrupted by the most restricted macrobiotic diets.

Implications for health

All types of diets, omnivorous and vegetarian alike, have potential health risks, as well as associated benefits.

In some studies, vegetarians have been shown to be more 'healthy' than meat-eaters, to suffer less from diseases such as heart disease, some cancers, hypertension and Type 2 diabetes, and to live longer. But this may be because of generally healthier lifestyles (i.e. not smoking, taking more exercise) and not just because meat is omitted from the diet. British vegetarians have been shown to have lower mortality rates than the general population, but a group of 'health conscious' non-vegetarians had a similarly lower death rate to the vegetarians in the study, showing that a healthier lifestyle overall may be the key to a longer life.

A vegetarian diet is certainly not automatically healthier than an omnivorous diet, and both can be healthy diets. Vegetarians and meat-eaters alike should aim for a balanced diet, which is low in fat (and especially saturates) and includes at least 5 portions of fruit and vegetables every day, coupled with a healthy lifestyle, which includes not smoking, being physically active and maintaining a sensible body weight.

Nutrition for vegetarians

To ensure a nutrition-ally balanced diet, a variety of foods should be selected from each of the food groups (see A balanced diet). If you are changing to a vegetarian diet, make sure that you do not simply cut out meat or other animal products: a vegetarian diet is not simply a change from meat and 2 veg to 'no meat' and 2 veg. You need to identify substitute foods that contain the nutrients previously provided by meat.

Protein

Protein from animal-derived food contains all of the amino-acids (protein 'building-blocks) that the body needs, and so a vegetarian diet that includes milk or egg protein is likely to contain enough high quality protein. Most plant food proteins (with the exception of soya) have a low content of one or more of the amino acids needed by the body (usually referred to as indispensable or essential amino acids). Furthermore, different ones are missing in different plant foods. Therefore, plant foods can be combined to provide high quality protein. Complementary combinations include:
⇨ Pulses/rice – bean casserole and rice, dhal and rice
⇨ Pulses/cereal – baked beans on toast
⇨ Nuts/cereal – peanut butter sandwich, nut roast

If the proteins from different plant sources are eaten together (or at least over a day), the amino acid profiles of the plant proteins will complement each other. Deficits in amino acids in any one plant protein will be compensated for by the amino acids in another. Thus if vegetarians and vegans eat a variety of vegetable proteins there is no reason why their intake of protein cannot be as good as that of a person who eats meat or other foods that contain animal protein.

Minerals

Serious deficiencies of minerals are not widespread in vegetarian populations. However, some people may be having suboptimal intakes of some minerals, especially those people who have recently changed to a vegetarian diet and may not be well informed about good food choices, or those 'new' vegetarians whose bodies have not had time to adapt to the poorer bioavailability of some minerals from plant foods.

Calcium

Vegetarians who consume milk and milk products are likely to have adequate intakes of calcium. However, some vegans may have low intakes of calcium as relatively few other foods contain large amounts, and the bioavailability of calcium from some plant sources may be greatly reduced by phytate or oxalate also present in the food. These substances can form complexes with the calcium which are insoluble and cannot be absorbed by the body. Where requirements for calcium are high (for example, during adolescence and during lactation) supplements containing calcium and calcium-fortified foods (such as fortified soya products) may be useful.

Iodine

Lacto-ovo-vegetarian diets usually contain adequate amounts of iodine, but vegans are at risk of low intakes. On the other hand, those who consume a lot of seaweed may have excessive intakes of iodine. Consumption of small amounts of iodised salt or seaweed is therefore advisable for those following a vegan diet to ensure sufficient intake.

Iron

Much of the easily-absorbed iron (haem iron) in omnivorous diets comes from red meat and offal. Plant foods contain no haem iron at all. Iron from non-haem sources such as eggs, cereal products, green vegetables, nuts and pulses is less well absorbed, but the presence of vitamin C from fruit, fruit juices and vegetables will enhance the absorption of non-haem iron; for example, having beans on toast and a glass of orange juice at the same meal. However, tea (because of tannins) and the plant substances phytate and oxalate reduce iron absorption.

Generally speaking, studies have shown that among vegetarians and vegans, iron intakes are similar to or higher than those of omnivores, but that iron stores in the body are usually lower, especially in female vegetarians. Provided sufficient iron is included in the diet, iron deficiency anaemia is not common amongst vegetarians and vegans, but iron deficiency anaemia has been reported in macrobiotic vegetarians who followed a very restrictive diet and consumed brown rice, which is rich in phytates, as their staple food.

Zinc

Foods considered to be the most abundant sources of this mineral include meat, poultry, dairy products, bread and other cereal products, and seafood. If many of these foods are excluded, dietary intake may be low but it is thought that adaptation to the diet might occur with time, resulting in an increase in the proportion of zinc absorbed from the intestine. Good plant sources of zinc include bread and cereal products, pulses, nuts and seeds, but many of these are also high in phytate, which is an inhibitor of zinc absorption. Although unrefined foods (e.g. wholemeal bread and brown rice) do contain more phytate, they are still preferable to refined sources, which contain less zinc and other micronutrients.

Vitamins

Most vitamins can be provided by foods of plant origin. However, vitamin B12 is found only in foods of animal origin, and there are few plant sources of vitamin D.

People follow a vegetarian diet for a variety of personal, philosophical, ecological and economical reasons

---

Vitamin B12

Although the body's requirement for vitamin B12 is only a few micrograms per day, it is essential that vegans, and other people who avoid all animal foods, include a source of vitamin B12 in their diet, either as a supplement (usually in tablet form) or as fortified foods (such as yeast extract, fortified soya milk or fortified breakfast cereal). Fermented products, such as tempeh and miso (obtained from fermented soya beans), shiitake mushrooms and algae (spirulina and nori) contain substances which are similar chemically to vitamin B12 but do not work in the body in the same way as the active vitamin. Therefore, these foods cannot be relied upon as sources of vitamin B12.

Vitamin D

Although previously thought to be rare in white people in Britain, low vitamin D status has been observed among older adults and some children. It is also been reported among the Asian population, particularly among children, adolescents women and the elderly, many of whom are vegetarian. Prolonged deficiency of vitamin D results in rickets in children and osteomalacia in adults. A combination of factors may be associated with low vitamin D status including:
⇨ low exposure to sunlight: this may be due to seclusion or strict dress codes limiting vitamin D synthesis in the skin.

⇨ type of vegetarian diet: vitamin D is found naturally in only a few foods, all of which are of animal origin, for example meat, oily fish such as mackerel and sardines, eggs, whole milk and its products. Some breakfast cereals, yoghurts and all margarines (required by law in the UK to contain vitamin D) and reduced fat spreads are fortified with vitamin D.

Those who receive little exposure to the sun have a greater need to ensure that they include dietary sources of vitamin D, and it is recommended that all young children, Asian women, and elderly people who are housebound or who live in an institution, take a vitamin D supplement in tablet form, to prevent the development of rickets and osteomalacia. An adequate intake of calcium is also important in bone development.

Animal and plant sources of vitamins and minerals

Protein

Animal sources: meat, poultry, fish, eggs, milk, cheese and yogurt
Plant sources: soya, pulses (including lentils, chick peas and beans, including baked beans), bread, grains, seeds, potatoes, nuts

Calcium

Animal sources: milk, cheese, yogurt and tinned sardines and salmon including the bones (the soft bones should not be discarded)
Plant sources: fortified soya milk and tofu, seeds (e.g. sesame seeds), green leafy vegetables (e.g. spring greens), nuts (e.g. almonds), bread (especially white bread), dried fruit (e.g. apricots)

Iron

Animal sources: liver, red meat, chicken, fish (haem iron), eggs (non-haem iron)
Plant sources: fortified breakfast cereals (the label should be checked to see if iron has been added), bread, pulses (e.g. soya beans), green vegetables, dried fruits (e.g. apricots), nuts, plain chocolate

Vitamin A

Animal sources: liver, butter, whole milk, cheese
Plant sources: yellow/orange vegetables (e.g. carrots) and dark leafy ones (e.g. parsley, watercress), yellow/orange fruit (e.g. mangoes, and apricots – fresh or dried), fortified margarines and spreads, sweet potato. NB. In vegetables and fruit, vitamin A is present in the form of carotenoids, e.g. beta-carotene

Vitamin B12

Animal sources: liver, meat, poultry, fish, milk and milk products, eggs
Plant sources: fortified products only (check on the label)

Vitamin D

Animal sources: oily fish, meat, whole milk and its products, fortified milk products (such as skimmed milk powder), eggs
Plant sources: fortified margarine and spreads, fortified breakfast cereals (the label should be checked to see if vitamin D has been added)

⇨ The above information is an extract from the BNF factsheet 'Vegetarian and Vegan Diets' and is reprinted with permission. Visit www.nutrition.org.uk for more information.

© British Nutrition Foundation

Going vegetarian

Information from the Vegetarian Society

Why become vegetarian?

There are as many reasons for becoming vegetarian as there are vegetarians; it's a highly personal and individual decision to make. But in a survey conducted on behalf of The Vegetarian Society the majority of people said that they gave up meat and fish because they did not morally approve of killing animals, or because they objected to the ways in which animals are kept, treated and killed for food.

With the growing awareness of the importance of healthy food, many people are also becoming vegetarian because it matches the kind of low fat, high fibre diet recommended by dieticians and doctors. Concern about the environment is another factor as people become more aware of the effect raising animals for their meat is having on the environment. Or you may be concerned about wasting world food resources by using land to raise animals for meat instead of growing crops that can feed more people directly.

Common questions about vegetarianism

Use these answers to some of the most common questions asked about vegetarianism to put at rest your own mind, or to respond to any queries from meat-eating friends.

What is a Vegetarian?
A vegetarian is someone who does not eat meat, fish, poultry or any slaughterhouse by-product such as gelatine. Vegetarians live on a diet of grains, pulses, nuts, seeds, vegetables and fruit, with or without free-range eggs, milk and milk products. Vegetarians not eating anything containing dairy products or eggs are called vegans.

Isn't it hard being a vegetarian?
Not at all. Vegetarian food is widely available in shops and restaurants, it's easy to cook and you're probably already eating many vegetarian meals such as beans on toast or jacket potato and cheese without even putting your mind to it. It's no sacrifice to give up meat when there are so many delicious recipes and so many tasty foods to experiment with. Plus you'll have the satisfaction of knowing that you're eating a healthy diet that doesn't involve the killing of animals or the abuse of the world's resources.

Where will I buy all this new food for my vegetarian diet?
Exactly the same place you used to buy food – in markets, supermarkets, corner shops. Vegetarian food, both in its 'raw state' as grains, pulses and vegetables, and as pre-cooked meals, is widely available nowadays.

Many people are becoming vegetarian because it matches the kind of low fat, high fibre diet recommended by dieticians and doctors

---

What do I say to my family/ friends?
Don't get caught up in arguments, just gather all the information about vegetarianism so you can calmly explain your decision. Then try introducing them to some of the delicious meat-free meals you're enjoying and see if you can win them over by setting a good example.

Aren't vegetarians being hypocritical because they still wear leather or exploit cows for their milk?
There is a very valid argument for becoming vegan – for giving up all dairy products, eggs and any other animal by-products. But realistically speaking, few people can go from being a meat eater to a vegan overnight. Vegetarianism is a very important halfway house. And even if you never go on to being vegan, you've already made an impact and saved the lives of many animals simply by giving up meat. Far from being hypocritical, you're making an effort to change the way you live for the better. How far you go with vegetarianism is up to you, but however small the step you take, it's not wasted. And don't feel that you have to become a perfect vegetarian overnight. If you forget to check the ingredients list and realise that you've just eaten something containing gelatine, don't feel that you've failed. Take it one step at a time and enjoy learning more about the vegetarian lifestyle. The important thing is that you're doing something!

Aren't all vegetarians pale and unhealthy?
This old stereotype has taken a long time to die out. In fact, people who follow a varied, well-balanced vegetarian diet are in line with the current nutritional recommendations for a low fat, high fibre diet. That's why medical studies are proving that vegetarians are less likely to suffer from such illnesses as heart disease, cancer, diet-related diabetes, obesity and high blood pressure. So, if for no other reason, go vegetarian as a favour to your body!

What happens if I have to try to get a vegetarian meal in a restaurant?
There are very few restaurants now that don't offer at least one vegetarian option. Vegetarianism is such a growing movement, restaurateurs can't afford to ignore it. In the unlikely event that a restaurant doesn't have anything for you, don't be put fobbed off, especially with the offer of a fish or chicken dish which are 'practically vegetarian' – they're not!! Simply ask politely if they can make something specially for you. if they can't be bothered, why give them the benefit of your custom when there are plenty of other places all too willing to help.

Isn't vegetarian food boring?
Vegetarians don't eke out a miserable existence on a few limp lettuce leaves

and some boiled rice. And a proper vegetarian meal doesn't mean taking the meat away and leaving the side vegetables. With the hundreds of different vegetables, grains, fruit, pulses and nuts and seeds that exist, you could live to be 100 without exhausting all the possibilities for imaginative, nutritious meals! And as vegetarian food tends to be cheaper than a meat-based diet, you can afford to treat yourself to more expensive delicacies such as asparagus.

Won't it take a long time to prepare the food?

Just because there are so many wonderful vegetarian dishes to try, doesn't mean you have to become an expert cook and spend hours in the kitchen. You can easily cook good, wholesome vegetarian meals in under half an hour, and don't forget that most manufacturers now also offer a wide range of ready-made vegetarian dishes.

But how will I get enough of the vital nutrients such as iron and protein?

A well-balanced vegetarian diet provides all the nutrients you need for good health. In the case of protein, it's not only found in meat. It's also present in adequate quantities in dairy products, eggs and nuts, as well as in combinations of foods such as pulses and grains. In fact it would be very difficult to design a vegetarian diet that doesn't include enough protein.

Useful tips on going and staying vegetarian

⇨ Treat yourself to a vegetarian cookbook for inspiration and advice. There are a wide range covering recipes for beginners, advanced cooks, slimmers, diabetics. Most also give dietary advice. (If you buy your books using our link to Amazon, the Society will benefit from your support).

⇨ Find our more about the subject. Our New Veggies Start Here section has information on all subjects relating to vegetarianism from the ethical issues to the practical day-to-day details, as well as being able to answer any other questions you might have.

⇨ Start gradually. Adapt familiar meals such as lasagne and shepherd's pie by using textured vegetable protein. Although fully vegetarian, it has the look, taste and texture of mince or meat chunks, according to which variety you buy. It is available from health food stores. If you don't buy the flavoured variety, be aware that you need to add seasoning of some kind or it will remain bland and uninteresting.

⇨ Buy vegetarian cheese. It's not an unfamiliar product as cheese is probably already on your shopping list. But whereas some cheeses are made with an ingredient from the stomachs of slaughtered calves, vegetarian cheese uses vegetable-derived rennet. Every supermarket now stocks at least one kind of vegetarian cheese, and many of the more unusual varieties such as Stilton and Brie are also now available in vegetarian versions.

⇨ Buy free-range eggs. Again, eggs are another staple ingredient in many people's diets so it won't take much effort to pick up the free-range variety instead of the Battery Produced.

⇨ Read the labels. Although you may get the odd shock when you realise that a food product that seems vegetarian in fact contains something such as gelatine or animal fat, there are plenty of others you'd be surprised and pleased to find out are suitable for you.

⇨ Look for The Vegetarian Society's Seedling Symbol on food products. It tells you at a glance that the product is suitable for vegetarians.

⇨ Pulses. Forget the dried variety if you find them difficult to prepare – go for the tinned variety of kidney beans, chick peas, etc.

⇨ Adapt familiar dishes. If you're the only vegetarian in your family and it's too difficult or expensive to cook totally separate meals, adapt a meat dish. A casserole, for instance, can be made with beans and vegetables in one pan. Then the meat can be cooked separately and given just to the meat eaters. Or use soya mince and see if anyone notices the difference.

Don't be put off by unfamiliar foods. Tofu, for instance, is a boon to vegetarians, especially new ones. This by-product of soya beans is incredibly versatile and easy to use. And if you use the plain variety, don't think that you've done something wrong when it appears tasteless in the finished recipe – it's meant to absorb the flavour of other ingredients. Or you can buy the smoked or marinated versions.

⇨ Explore health food stores. They'll have vegetarian products you haven't seen before, and the assistants will be able to answer your questions about products suitable for your new lifestyle.

⇨ If you are in the UK, see The Shopping Hub Page on the Vegetarian Society website for local shops, restaurants etc.

What you should eat every day on a vegetarian diet

⇨ 3 or 4 servings of cereals/grains or potatoes

⇨ 4 or 5 servings of fruit and vegetables

⇨ 2 or 3 servings of pulses, nuts & seeds

⇨ 2 servings of milk, cheese, eggs or soya products

⇨ A small amount of vegetable oil and margarine or butter.

⇨ Some yeast extract such as Marmite, fortified with vitamin B12.

⇨ The above information is reprinted with kind permission from the Vegetarian Society. Visit www.vegsoc.org for more information.

© Vegetarian Society

Vegetarian and vegan

The important thing to remember if you're a vegetarian is that you need to eat a balanced diet to make sure you're getting all the nutrients your body needs

Healthy eating

The main healthy eating messages are the same for everybody. We should all be trying to do the following:

⇨ eating at least five portions of a variety of fruit and veg every day

⇨ basing meals on starchy foods such as pasta, rice, cereals and pulses such as beans, peas and lentils. These should make up about a third of the diet

⇨ eating some protein foods such as dairy products, eggs or pulses and having a variety of these foods

⇨ trying to grill, bake, poach, boil, steam, dry-fry or microwave instead of frying or roasting in oil

⇨ cutting down on sugar

⇨ watching how much salt we're eating – it's a good idea to check food labels and try not to add salt to your food when you're cooking

⇨ drinking about 1.2 litres (6 to 8 glasses) of fluid a day or more if you exercise

But you also need to make sure you're getting enough nutrients, especially protein, iron and selenium, which can sometimes be lacking in a meat-free diet.

Getting the nutrients you need
Getting enough protein

It's important to make sure you're getting enough protein.

These foods are all good sources, so try to include a mixture of these in your diet each day, and vary the types you choose:

⇨ pulses (such as lentils and beans)
⇨ nuts and seeds
⇨ eggs
⇨ soya and soya products such as tofu
⇨ mycoprotein, sold as Quorn™
⇨ wheat proteins, such as cereals, bread, rice and maize
⇨ milk and dairy products

Protein is made of amino acids, some of which are known as 'essential amino acids' because the body can't make them itself.

It's important to get some of each of these essential amino acids at the same time. But, only meat, poultry, fish and eggs contain the complete mix of essential amino acids.

This sounds complicated, but it's actually easy to get all the essential amino acids you need by eating different types of protein foods at the same time, in fact you will often being doing this already, for example by having:

⇨ beans on your toast
⇨ milk with your breakfast cereal
⇨ rice with lentil dhal
⇨ a rice and bean salad
⇨ vegetable chilli (with kidney beans) served with rice or tortillas
⇨ bread and cheese
⇨ soup made with lentils, beans or split peas with a chunk of bread
⇨ houmous and pitta bread

It's also not a good idea to rely on one type of protein because you might be missing out on nutrients. And, if for example you rely on cheese as your source of protein, you might be having too much saturated fat.

If you don't eat milk and dairy products, choose soya, rice or oat drinks fortified with calcium instead.

Getting enough iron

Although meat is the best source of iron, it can also be found in:

⇨ pulses
⇨ green vegetables such as watercress, broccoli, spring greens and okra
⇨ bread
⇨ fortified breakfast cereals

Remember that it's easier to absorb iron from food if we eat it with foods that contain vitamin C, so have some fruit or veg, or a glass of fruit juice with your meal.

Avoid drinking tea or coffee with your meals because these make it harder for the body to absorb iron. It's best to wait at least half an hour after eating before you have a tea or coffee.

Getting enough selenium

It's important to make sure you're getting enough selenium because selenium is important for our immune systems to function properly.

Meat, fish and nuts are the best sources of selenium, so if you're a strict vegetarian, it's important to make sure you're eating enough nuts.

Brazil nuts are a particularly good source of selenium, so try to eat a couple every day. Eating a small bag of mixed unsalted nuts can be a convenient way to get your daily selenium intake, but make sure it contains Brazils.

Bread and eggs also provide some selenium.

If you eat a mostly vegetarian diet but also eat fish, you should be getting enough selenium.

What do vegetarians eat?

Vegetarians don't eat any meat, fish, seafood or animal by-products such as gelatine, but the majority of vegetarians do eat some animal products, mainly milk, cheese and eggs.

Some people eat a mostly vegetarian diet, but also eat fish.

What do vegans eat?

Vegans don't eat any foods of animal origin. This includes meat, fish and dairy foods, and also honey.

If you are a vegan, you need to make sure you're getting enough protein and iron (see above), but it can also be difficult to get enough vitamin B12.

These are good vegan sources of vitamin B12:

⇨ yeast extract
⇨ fortified bread
⇨ fortified breakfast cereals

⇨ The above information is reprinted with kind permission from the Food Standards Agency. Visit www.eatwell.gov.uk for more information.

© Crown copyright

What makes a vegetarian?

Information from the Nestle Social Research Programme

People become vegetarian for three main reasons: health, taste or ethics. These reflect different values and motives for avoiding flesh. Amongst the young people there are different degrees of flesh avoidance. Two useful categories emerged. The kinds of food that people might choose not to eat include red meat, white meat, and fish. The category 'flesh-avoider' comprises anyone who excludes any of those products from their diet (in whatever combination). Of those who answered the question (97% of the sample) 44% are 'flesh-avoiders', and 56% are 'flesh-eaters'. 39% of boys and 50 % of girls are classified as 'flesh-avoiders'.

'Flesh-avoiders' by this criterion, are not strictly vegetarian in the accepted sense. A narrower category, 'vegetarian' comprises only those who exclude meat, or meat in combination with fish. Of the flesh-avoiders, 28.6% exclude red meat only, 44% exclude fish only, and 21.4% exclude red meat in combination with fish and/or white meat. This latter group constitutes the conventional definition of 'vegetarian', and they comprise 9.45% of the total sample.

There are considerable differences between flesh-avoiders and flesh-eaters on a number of values and attitudes. This suggests a somewhat differing worldview and a heightened awareness of some health and food-related issues.

The eating-related items on which flesh-avoiders differ from flesh-eaters include ethical, health and taste items. Unsurprisingly, they like the taste of meat less than do flesh-eaters. They are also more likely to regard not eating red meat as healthier. The 'ethical' items with which flesh-avoiders agree more than flesh-eaters include not liking the thought of eating meat, and not thinking it is right to kill animals for food.

Flesh-avoiders are more likely to pay attention to calories, eat organic food, and avoid food that might give them spots. They also eat more fresh fruit and vegetables.

Flesh-avoiders also differ from flesh-eaters on other areas of health and exercise. They worry more frequently about their health. They are generally less comfortable about exercising, and how they look in exercise clothes, and more reluctant to become too bulky or muscular. They are more likely to agree that 'exercising would be too much effort'. They would prefer more to dance or do yoga – especially girls. However, they enjoy the competition of exercising more than do flesh-eaters.

Given these clear differences in health values and motives between flesh-avoiders and flesh-eaters, what is distinctive about the specific group of true vegetarians? In particular, is fish-avoidance in the same ethical or taste domain as meat avoidance? In contrast to those who avoid meat, those who avoid fish only (but not meat) are significantly less concerned about the taste of meat, the thought of eating meat, and whether avoiding red meat is healthier. They are less concerned about killing animals for food, and about the conditions under which animals are reared. This suggests that those who only exclude fish, but not meat, from their diet are more concerned about taste than ethics.

However, fish-avoiders in combination with meat-avoiders comprise the large group of flesh-avoiders, who significantly differ from flesh-eaters in terms of their awareness of and sensitivity to health issues.

⇨ The above information is taken from the report 'My Body, My Self' from the Nestlé Social Research Programme and is reprinted with permission. Visit www.spreckley.co.uk/nestle/reports.htm for more information.

© Nestlé

Young people's values about food

Differences between 'Flesh-avoiders' and 'Flesh-eaters' in relation to values about food, and reasons for exercising or not – mean scores.

Scale: 1 = agree strongly. 2 = agree slightly. 3 = neither agree nor disagree. 4 = disagree slightly. 5 = disagree strongly.	Flesh-avoiders		Flesh-eaters	
Values and Food (QC19)	Males (Base 138)	Females (Base 158)	Males (Base 216)	Females (Base 157)
I think it is healthier not to eat red meat	2.00	2.11	2.72	2.65
It's against my religion to eat certain foods	2.21	2.55	2.73	2.79
I would prefer to eat less meat than I do now	2.29	2.24	2.93	2.74
I try to eat organic food	2.35	2.30	2.64	2.87
I try to avoid food that would give me spots	2.51	2.53	2.75	2.89
I don't like the thought of eating meat	2.72	2.32	3.93	3.80
I don't like the taste of meat	2.94	2.48	3.60	3.43
I don't think it's right to kill animals for food	3.10	2.70	3.90	3.63
I pay attention to the calories in the food I eat	3.12	3.08	3.74	3.10

Base: All young people aged 11-21 for whom data are available (669), April-May 2004. Source: Nestle Social Research Programme/MORI.

Vegetarians can cut cancer risk

Information from the Vegetarian Society

In a world where every day, week and month seems to be branded by a dozen different causes, campaigns or brands, the organisers of National Vegetarian Week are welcoming the happy coincidence which sees Cancer Prevention Week fall alongside this year's seven-day celebration of the diet that best fits the World Cancer Research Fund's suggested regime for reducing your cancer risk.

The fourteenth National Vegetarian Week (Monday 22 to Sunday 28 May) is organised by national charity, The Vegetarian Society. The week seeks to raise the profile of vegetarianism and of the free support and guidance which the Society offers all year round to vegetarians and those considering vegetarianism.

'Vegetarians are far more likely than any other group in society to be eating five portions of fruit and vegetables every day'

The World Cancer Research Fund (WCRF) urges anyone seeking to reduce their cancer risk 'to choose a diet rich in a variety of plant-based foods; to eat plenty of vegetables and fruits and to maintain a healthy weight'.

According to The Vegetarian Society's Information Manager, Chris Olivant, 'Vegetarians are far more likely than any other group in society to be eating the government's recommended five portions of fruit and vegetables every day. We also tend to eat a greater variety of grains, pulses, nuts, seeds and other plant-based foods than meat-eaters.'

Beyond the direct impact of diet, obesity is known to contribute to a person's risk of developing cancer as well as heart disease and diabetes. A study recently published in the International Journal of Obesity confirmed that vegetarians gain less weight than meat-eaters as they grow older. *23 May 2006*

The above information is reprinted with kind permission from the Vegetarian Society. Visit www.vegsoc.org for more information.

© *Vegetarian Society*

Questions to think about

Information from the British Humanist Association

⇨ A rabbit is born and lives its whole life in a small barren cage. Does it make any difference to your moral views on this if it is kept (a) as a pet, (b) for meat, (c) for fur, (d) for medical experiments, (e) for beauty product experiments.

⇨ Do you think that animals have a different attitude to death from humans?

⇨ Is eating "free range meat" an adequate response to a moral concern about the way we use land? Is eating less or no meat a better response?

⇨ How consistent are you in your attitudes to animals? Do you tolerate some uses of animals and not others? Do you kill wasps and flies? Do you eat factory-farmed meat or chicken? Do you know how meat gets to your table? Should we all be vegetarians?

⇨ Do some animals matter more than others? Do you think there should be some kind of sliding scale of concern?

With thanks to Dr Georgia Mason of Oxford University Department of Zoology

⇨ The above information is an extract from the British Humanist Association's factsheet 'A Humanist Discussion of Vegetarianism' and is reprinted with permission. Visit www.humanism.org.uk for more information.

© *British Humanist Association*

Vegetarianism and IQ

Children with a high IQ are more likely to become vegetarian

Intelligent children may be more likely to be vegetarian as adults, suggests a University of Southampton-led study published online by the British Medical Journal today.

The study led by Dr Catharine Gale of the University's MRC Epidemiology Resource Centre looked to see why people with higher IQs appeared to be less likely to suffer from heart disease.

Recent evidence suggests that vegetarianism may be linked to lower cholesterol levels and a reduced risk of obesity and heart disease

---

'We examined the records of 8179 men and women aged 30 years, whose IQ had been tested at the age of ten. Twenty years on, 366 (4.5 per cent) of participants said they were vegetarian. Of these, 9 (2.5 per cent) were vegan and 123 (33.6 per cent) stated they were vegetarian but reported eating fish or chicken,' says Dr Gale.

'Those who were vegetarian by the age of 30 had scored five IQ points above average at the age of ten. This can be partly accounted for by better education and higher occupational social class, but it remained statistically significant after adjusting for these factors.'

Recent evidence suggests that vegetarianism may be linked to lower cholesterol levels and a reduced risk of obesity and heart disease. This might help to explain why children who score higher on intelligence tests tend to have a lower risk of coronary heart disease in later life.

'One explanation for the link between higher IQ and vegetarianism may be that brighter children grow up to think more about what they eat, which in some cases has led them to become vegetarians,' continues Dr Gale.

Professor Ian Deary from the University of Edinburgh, one of the study's co-authors, adds: 'As the only member of the research team who has never been a vegetarian I feel bound to emphasise that the link we have found might not be causal. Becoming vegetarian might be one of a number of more or less arbitrary cultural choices that clever people make, some of which might be beneficial to health, and some not.'

Vegetarians were also more likely to be female, to be of higher occupational social class and to have higher academic or vocational qualifications than non-vegetarians, although these differences were not reflected in their annual income, which was similar to that of non-vegetarians.

There was no difference in IQ score between strict vegetarians and those who said they were vegetarian but who reported eating fish or chicken.

Notes

1. The study can be viewed at http://www.bmj.com/cgi/rapidpdf/bmj.39030.675069.55

2. The study authors were:
   Dr Catharine Gale, Senior Research Fellow, Medical Research Council, Environmental Epidemiology Centre, University of Southampton (UK)
   Professor Ian Deary, Department of Psychology, University of Edinburgh
   Professor Ingrid Schoon, Department of Psychology, City University
   Dr David Batty, Wellcome Fellow, University of Glasgow MRC Social and Public Health Sciences Unit

15 December 2006

⇨ The above information is reprinted with kind permission from the University of Southampton. For more information, please visit the University of Southampton website at www.soton.ac.uk

© *University of Southampton*

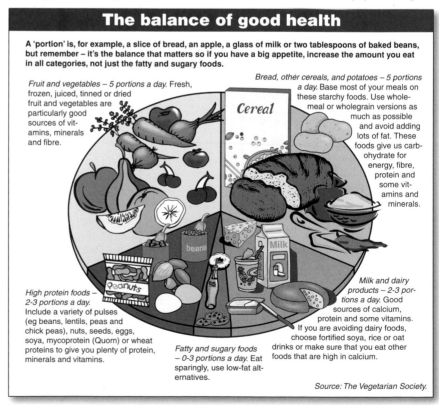

The balance of good health

A 'portion' is, for example, a slice of bread, an apple, a glass of milk or two tablespoons of baked beans, but remember – it's the balance that matters so if you have a big appetite, increase the amount you eat in all categories, not just the fatty and sugary foods.

Fruit and vegetables – 5 portions a day. Fresh, frozen, juiced, tinned or dried fruit and vegetables are particularly good sources of vitamins, minerals and fibre.

Bread, other cereals, and potatoes – 5 portions a day. Base most of your meals on these starchy foods. Use wholemeal or wholegrain versions as much as possible and avoid adding lots of fat. These foods give us carbohydrate for energy, fibre, protein and some vitamins and minerals.

High protein foods – 2-3 portions a day. Include a variety of pulses (eg beans, lentils, peas and chick peas), nuts, seeds, eggs, soya, mycoprotein (Quorn) or wheat proteins to give you plenty of protein, minerals and vitamins.

Fatty and sugary foods – 0-3 portions a day. Eat sparingly, use low-fat alternatives.

Milk and dairy products – 2-3 portions a day. Good sources of calcium, protein and some vitamins. If you are avoiding dairy foods, choose fortified soya, rice or oat drinks or make sure that you eat other foods that are high in calcium.

Source: The Vegetarian Society.

Vegetarian nutrition

Information from the British Nutrition Foundation

The number of people in the UK who claim to be vegetarian has increased dramatically during the last half century; statistics from the Second World War suggest that 0.2% of the population were vegetarian in the 1940s and it is estimated that, in 2000, between 3 and 7% of the population were vegetarian.

There is much interest in the potential effects of plant-based diets on a range of health outcomes and nutrition. A range of dietary practices followed by vegetarians has been identified, from the strict guidelines of the most restrictive macrobiotic diets, through vegan and lacto-ovo-vegetarian diets, to those that occasionally include fish or even chicken. The type of vegetarian diet followed by an individual may reflect the motive to be vegetarian; motives for being vegetarian include, amongst others, ethical and ecological issues, health concerns, sensory and taste preferences and philosophical teachings.

In addition to dietary choice patterns, vegetarians may differ from meat-eaters in a range of lifestyle behaviours: smoking habits, alcohol consumption, activity and leisure patterns and use of alternative therapies are all cited as examples. Furthermore, the body mass indices of vegetarians and vegans are typically 1-2 kg/m2 lower than matched omnivores. It is, therefore, important to remember this complex web of dietary and non-dietary differences when interpreting the results of studies comparing vegetarians with meat eaters, as such comparisons are not straightforward.

In terms of nutrient intakes, the key nutritional issue for vegetarians and vegans is whether the nutrients supplied by meat and fish, in an omnivorous diet, can be provided in adequate amounts in foods that are acceptable to vegetarians and vegans. In the UK, for example, meat and meat products provide a major contribution to intakes of protein, iron, zinc, vitamin B12 and vitamin D. Conversely, compared with omnivorous diets, plant-based diets are reported to contain more folate, fibre, antioxidants, phytochemicals and carotenoids. Vegans, however, may have low intakes of vitamin B12, vitamin D, calcium and iodine. UK studies comparing lacto-ovo-vegetarians, vegans, fish-eaters and meat-eaters have shown that lacto-ovo-vegetarians and vegans obtained a considerably lower proportion of dietary energy from total fat and saturated fatty acids (saturates), vegetarians and meat-eaters alike are advised to limit their intake of atherogenic saturates.

There is much interest in the potential effects of plant-based diets on a range of health outcomes and nutrition

---

A well-planned, balanced vegetarian or vegan diet can be nutritionally adequate, although more extreme diets, such as strict macrobiotic and raw food diets, are often low in energy and a range of micronutrients, making them wholly inadequate and inappropriate for children. Weaning onto a vegetarian diet follows the same principles as weaning onto an omnivorous diet, although care must be taken to ensure that a vegan diet is sufficiently energy and nutrient-dense for children. Studies of UK vegetarian and vegan children have revealed that their growth and development are within the normal range.

A number of studies have attempted to determine whether being vegetarian confers any protective effect, in terms of mortality and morbidity, from a range of chronic diseases. Evidence from a few large cohort studies suggests that vegetarians have lower overall mortality ratios than the general population, but this is not the case when vegetarians are compared with similar non-vegetarian groups who follow a health-conscious lifestyle. Vegetarianism has been associated with a reduction in several of the established risk factors for coronary heart disease (CHD), including more favourable blood lipid profile, lower body mass index and lower blood pressure. However, some studies suggest that vegetarians and vegans may be at greater risk of having raised plasma homocysteine levels, an emerging risk factor for cardiovascular disease.

Although a high intake of plant-derived foods has been linked with a reduced risk of certain cancers, there are no clear and consistent patterns of cancer incidence and mortality between vegetarians and meat-eaters. However, several studies have reported increased risk of colorectal cancer among those with the highest intakes of meat and the lowest intakes of dietary fibre, but there is no evidence that being vegetarian per se confers a protective effect.

More research is needed to establish whether vegetarianism has a role to play in protection against a range of other diseases that are less prevalent amongst vegetarian populations; lifestyle as well as nutritional differences will need to be taken into consideration. Following a vegetarian diet does not automatically equate to being healthier; vegetarians and meat-eaters alike need to be mindful of making appropriate dietary and lifestyle choices.

⇨ The above information is reprinted with kind permission from the British Nutrition Foundation. Visit www.nutrition.org.uk for more information.

Red meat

Juliette Kellow's red meat superfood facts

There might not be an official definition for the term super-food, but it's fair to say that when eaten as part of a balanced, varied diet, lean red meat is certainly up there on the list of superfoods. Lean red meat contains a variety of different nutrients, including protein, heart-healthy monounsaturates and omega3 fats, plus a wide variety of vitamins and minerals. And better still, it has nothing added or taken away and is naturally low in salt and free from additives.

Because red meat contains a wide range of nutrients, it's often called a nutrient-dense food – in other words, it contains a lot of nutrients in a relatively small amount of the food. Indeed, a recent report from the British Nutrition Foundation (Red Meat in the Diet) highlights that red meat includes many nutrients that are important for good health, including protein, iron, zinc, selenium, vitamin B12 and vitamin D. This is important because many adults have low intakes of these nutrients in their diet and so are at risk of becoming deficient in that nutrient.

Here are some key points regarding the superfood benefits of lean red meat:

⇨ Red meat is an important source of iron, needed for healthy blood and to prevent anaemia. Currently a quarter of females aged 1964 in the UK have iron intakes below the minimum amount to stay healthy. Meanwhile, 40% of women under the age of 34 have seriously low intakes of iron and so are putting themselves at risk of anaemia. Teenage girls are also at risk of anaemia as they have higher iron requirements due to menstruation – around half of all 11-18 year old girls have iron intakes below the minimum amount recommended for good health.

⇨ The type of iron in beef (haem iron) is more easily absorbed and used by the body than the iron in plant foods (nonhaem iron). This makes beef a great choice for children. Numerous studies show even a mild deficiency of iron can affect a child's learning ability, while boosting intakes improves behaviour, concentration, mental sharpness and cognitive development.

⇨ According to a study in the journal Pediatrics children and teenagers deficient in iron are more likely to be overweight due to overall poor eating habits. Furthermore, children with poor iron stores may feel constantly tired and therefore be less active, which can promote weight gain.

⇨ The iron found in red meat is in a form that the body can use more easily than the iron found in plant foods such as pulses, nuts, seeds and leafy green veg.

⇨ Red meat is a good source of vitamin B12. This vitamin only occurs naturally in animal foods. Studies show that vitamin B12 intakes are consistently lower in vegetarians and particularly vegans, indicating that meat makes an important contribution to intakes of this vitamin.

⇨ Red meat contains selenium. This nutrient is an important antioxidant, which has been linked to reducing the risk of heart disease and certain cancers.

⇨ Red meat contains protein, which helps to improve satiety and fills us up for longer. This makes protein-rich foods excellent for helping us to control our weight so that we don't become over-weight or obese.

⇨ Red meat contains small amounts of omega3 fats, which help to keep the heart healthy. With the exception of oil-rich fish, few foods contain good amounts of omega3s. This makes the small amounts in red meat an important source, especially for people who eat little or no oily fish.

⇨ Red meat has become substantially lower in fat in recent years with the fat content having been reduced by more than 30 percent for pork, 15 percent for beef and 10 percent for lamb. Lean beef now contains just 5 percent fat, lamb 8 percent fat and pork just 4 percent fat.

⇨ It's a myth that red meat is packed with saturates. At least half the fat in lean red meat is heart-healthy monounsaturated and polyunsaturated fats. Choos-ing lean cuts of meat and trimming off any visible fat helps to reduce the saturated fat content further.

⇨ The above information is re-printed with kind permission from the Meat and Livestock Commission. Visit www.meatmatters.com for more information.

© Meat and Livestock Commission

Eat less meat – it's costing the earth

Information from Compassion in World Farming

Why eat less meat?

The simple answer to the question 'why eat less meat?' is that we're eating too much already – too much for our own good, for the long-term sustainability of the planet – and for animal welfare.

Background

Globally, meat consumption is increasing at a phenomenal rate. In the last 40 years, consumption has grown from 56 to 89 kilos of meat per person, per year in Europe and from 89 to 124 kilos in the US. Forty years ago, the Chinese were eating only 4 kilos of meat pp/pa – that figure has now reached 54 kilos and is still rising.

This global increase is a huge threat to us all.

Human health

Meat, meat products and dairy foods make up the greatest percentage of saturated fat in the average 'western' diet, contributing significantly to the huge increases in obesity, adult onset diabetes, heart disease and certain cancers. One of the world's leading nutritionists, Professor Walter Willett, of Harvard School of Public Health, lists the adverse health effects of high meat consumption (particularly red meat): 'higher rates of several important cancers ...heart disease and type 2 diabetes.'

Feeding the world

The majority of farm animals globally are fed on imported soya and cereals – globally between a third and a half of the world's harvest is fed to animals. Yet much of the nutritional value of the feed is lost in its 'conversion' to meat. It takes 10 kilos of feed to produce 1 kilo of beef, 5 kilos for a kilo of pork.

In a world of increasing water scarcity, we know that it takes 100,000 litres of water to produce

CIWF
TRUST

a kilo of beef, yet only 900 litres to produce a kilo of wheat.

Environmental damage

Farm animals produce 13 billion tonnes of waste every year. Liquid effluent from factory farms often pollutes soils and rivers, gaseous wastes like methane and carbon dioxide contribute to global warming.

Animal welfare

Whilst in the UK and EU we have made great strides in phasing out some of the worst factory farming systems, globally, factory farming is increasing rapidly to meet the growing demand for meat. In the US, most meat is from highly intensive systems. Agribusiness companies from the US, Canada and Europe are investing in pig and chicken factory farms in countries like China. So the global burden of farm animal suffering is on the increase.

Eat less meat

In response to this global crisis, CIWF has launched an important campaign to persuade people to eat less meat – and when they buy meat, to buy preferably organic or free-range meat produced in sustainable farming systems.

Our prime target is the wealthy western world where meat consumption is at its peak. If we can make reducing meat consumption a real policy issue, then hopefully developing countries will learn from our bitter experience and avoid the policies which have promoted meat production and consumption here for so many years, with such disastrous impacts on our health, on the animals and on the environment.

Call on individuals

CIWF is calling on individuals to reduce their consumption of meat and buy only organic and free range meat.

Call on governments

CIWF is calling on western governments and global food and farming bodies to set targets for at least a 15% reduction in meat consumption by 2020.

⇨ The above information is reprinted with kind permission from Compassion in World Farming. Visit www.ciwf.org.uk for more information.

© Compassion in World Farming

Meat eaters care but carry on regardless...

Information from the Vegetarian Society

The fourteenth National Vegetarian Week, sponsored by Quorn, begins tomorrow and with research showing that meat eaters and vegetarians share many of the same attitudes towards animals, The Vegetarian Society is asking why some people commit to a cruelty-free lifestyle while others carry on eating meat.

Vegetarians are considered to be, variously, compassionate, squeamish and just plain fussy but surveys show that their attitude towards the rearing and killing of animals for food varies very little from those of the majority, meat-eating population.

Surveys show that vegetarians' attitude towards the rearing and killing of animals for food varies very little from those of the majority, meat-eating population

---

Disgust at the treatment of farm animals was the number one reason vegetarians gave for both going and remaining vegetarian in a survey carried out on The Vegetarian Society's website. Meanwhile, a GfK NOP poll commissioned by the Society showed that, despite 95% of respondents saying they were not a vegetarian, only 13% agreed with the statement 'I don't really care what happens to farm animals'. Half admitted to feeling sorry for farm animals, while 35% were horrified by the way they are treated. Yet the vast majority of these respondents continue to eat meat on a regular basis. The Vegetarian Society is now asking, why?

'The survey results are very comforting in a way, because they show that most people do care,' commented Tina Fox, Chief Executive of The Vegetarian Society. 'However, they also show a huge gap between attitudes and action. It is hard to find someone who actually defends factory-farming practices these days, yet the vast majority of men, women and children in the UK still eat the results every day. I find it difficult to understand why.'

Alongside moral and spiritual beliefs, vegetarians also rated the avoidance of hypocrisy as an important reason for living without meat, agreeing with statements including 'I wouldn't eat cat or dog, so it makes no sense to discriminate against other animals' and 'I couldn't kill an animal myself so I can't expect someone else to do it for me'. Concurring with this view, only 4% of respondents to the NOP poll would eat meat from a cat or a dog, while two-thirds (82% of women) would not kill an animal for their own plate.

The Vegetarian Society's Head of Communications, Liz O'Neill, finds it hard to explain why some people believe that animal cruelty makes it wrong to eat meat, while others carry on regardless. 'Vegetarianism is far more evenly spread throughout the population than many people think, so social, gender and age differences don't explain it. We are the oldest vegetarian organisation in the world, but we don't understand why so many people appear to share our views but not our commitment. If anyone can explain it to me, I would be happy to listen.'

NOP GfK Telebus poll of 1,000 people was carried out in March 2005. Results were weighted in order to be nationally representative. *19 May 2006*

⇨ The above information is reprinted with kind permission from the Vegetarian Society. Visit www.vegsoc.org for more information.
© *Vegetarian Society*

Nutrients found in red meat				
Vitamin A	Essential for healthy bones, skin and eyes. Strengthens the immune system.	Chromium	Required to metabolise sugar and and regulated action of insulin.
Vitamin B₁ (Thiamine)	Supports energy production, helps heart, digestive and nervous systems to function.	Copper	Helps with red blood cell production and lung function.
Vitamin B₂ (Riboflavin)	Supports energy production, essential for formation of red blood cells, healthy skin, hair and nails + helps precent cataracts.	Folic acid	Essential for growth and division of cells, red blood cell information.
Vitamin B₃ (Niacin)	Helps digestive and nervous systems function. Helps healthy skin and red blood cell count. Essential for energy metabolism.	Iron	Carries oxygen from lungs to tissues around body, deficiency can cause anaemia.
Vitamin B₅	Helps to maintain healthy skin.	Long-chain n-3 fatty acids	Can help protect the heart.
Vitamin B₆	Helps digestive and nervous systems function. Essential for healthy red blood cells and maintains fluid balance.	Magnesium	Keeps heart and liver healthy, essential for strong bones and good muscle function.
Vitamin B₁₂	Helps red blood cells + bone marrow form. Helps maintain healthy cardiovascualar + nervous systems..	Potassium	Maintains fluid and electrolyte balance in body. Diets high in potassium can help reduce hypertension.
Vitamin D	Essential for bone development and healthy heart. Helps to metabolise calcium.	Selenium	Plays a role in regulating the thyroid gland. Has antioxidant properties.
Zinc	Essential for healthy skin, bones, teeth, immune and reproductive systems, liver function, sense of smell and taste.	Vitamin K	Regulates blood clotting.

Source: Meat and Livestock Commission

Brits go wild for game

Information from Mintel

The British are taking a walk on the wild side, as we get a real taste for game*. Latest research from MINTEL shows that sales for meat such as venison, pheasant and grouse soared 46% between 2004 and 2006, to reach £57 million last year. Although still a premium, niche market, these meats are clearly a cut above the rest, with everyday red meat and poultry markets growing by no more than 5% over the same two year period.

'The market for game is growing strongly as we increasingly look for exciting, alternative flavours that fit with our renewed interest in good quality food. But game also has a surprising fan in health conscious Brits. These meats are low in fat and cholesterol, but are still full of flavour and this healthy image is definitely helping to boost sales, especially amongst women,' comments David Bird, senior market analyst at MINTEL.

Looking to the future, the popularity of game shows no sign of abating, with sales set to increase by a further 47% to hit £84 million by 2011. With this growing interest in game, coupled with the rise of farmers' markets and locally produced food – bringing us closer to the natural source of our food – it is not too hard to imagine a possible revival of activities such as fishing and shooting. Indeed, an unexpected hero has emerged in the form of W M W Fowler, with his Countryman's Cookbook fast becoming a best-seller. Although it was a flop back when it was first published more than 40 years ago, his descriptions of not only how to cook game but also how to shoot, skin, pluck and gut it, have clearly struck a chord with today's modern cooks.

Flying off the shelves

Taking almost half (47%) of game sales, it is venison that has really captured the nation's imagination. The market for venison has come on leaps and bounds since the days when it was only available as a roasting joint. Today, you can enjoy venison burgers, sausages and steaks, all without the fat of regular pork or beef varieties. Pheasant, partridge and grouse make up almost a third (31%) of game sales, while 'other game', such as hare and wild boar, complete the sector, with 22% of sales.

'Today's growing concern about the environment and the negative impact of mass produced food is changing the types of food we buy, with many of us opting for food that is organic, locally sourced or bought from a farmers' market. As game comes from free ranging animals and is wild and natural, this market is clearly perfectly placed to take full advantage of this trend,' explains David Bird.

It's 'game on' for game

Game is now moving away from being a treat on the odd special occasion, to a meal that is enjoyed on a much more regular basis. Indeed, four in ten (41%) Brits now eat game, with a further 12% ready to give it a go.

'Game is now more readily available than ever before, with improved standards of handling and hygiene having encouraged supermarkets to stock game. Distribution has also improved considerably over the last couple of years and the popularity of these meats amongst top chefs around the country has meant that many more people are getting to taste the likes of venison, partridge and grouse. People are clearly becoming more adventurous and are prepared to give these meats a go,' comments David Bird.

* Game – includes grouse, guinea fowl, pheasant, partridge, wood pigeon, wild duck, venison, wild boar, rabbit, hare, snipe and woodcock.

About Mintel

Mintel is a worldwide leader of competitive media, product and consumer intelligence. For more than 35 years, Mintel has provided key insight into leading global trends. With offices in Chicago, London, Belfast and Sydney, Mintel's innovative product line provides unique data that has a direct impact on client success. For more information on Mintel, please visit their Web site at www.mintel.com. *February 2007*

⇨ The above information is reprinted with kind permission from Mintel. Visit www.mintel.com for more information.

© Mintel

Happy hunting

Vegetarians have long claimed the moral high ground. But meat-eating can be ethical and sustainable, says Tristram Stuart – if you're willing to get your hands dirty

In 1782, the Scottish soldier John Oswald arrived in Bombay eager to fight for the East India Company. But after witnessing Britain's savage treatment of the natives, Oswald quit his post and went on a walkabout among the Indians. Under the influence of his newfound Hindu hosts, Oswald cast aside the haggis and roast beef of his homeland and converted to vegetarianism. With ideological fervour he attacked the human oppressors who were guilty of exploiting both humans and animals alike. In his own country, he realised, the Scottish Highlanders were being forcefully evicted by the meat-gorging rich in a greedy quest to provide their animals with more grazing.

Vegetarianism and veganism remain powerful protests against modern society's disregard for the interests of other animals

---

By the time Oswald finally returned to Britain, he had become, according to one contemporary, 'a convert so much to the Hindu faith, that the ferocity of the young soldier of fortune sunk into the mild philosophic manners of the Hindoo Brahmin'. Oswald's next career move was to join the French Revolution with a proclamation that the republican fraternité should be extended to the animal kingdom, before grape-shot laid him and his utopian dreams to rest.

Oswald was one of many revolutionary vegetarians, from the 18th century to the 21st, who imbibed the philosophy of Jean-Jacques Rousseau. In 1755, Rousseau had argued that because animals shared with humans the capacity for sensation, they at least had the right to be protected from 'unnecessary' maltreatment. The majority, meanwhile, maintained that animals had no value except insofar as they were useful to humans. In Jewish and Christian societies, this animal-unfriendly view had been bolstered by the Bible's testimony of God's words to Noah: 'the fear of you and the dread of you shall be upon every beast of the earth ... Every moving thing that liveth shall be meat for you' (Genesis, 9:2-3).

Two-and-a-half centuries after Rousseau's declaration, vegetarians and carnivores are still locked in battle. But there is a pressing case for these warring camps to lay aside their differences and unite against a problem that affects us all. For one of the greatest threats to the welfare of animals, to biodiversity and to humans comes from the same single source: the perverse state of the modern meat industry. Viewed from a holistic ecological perspective, some meat -such as conscientiously hunted animals – involves less suffering and environmental damage than arable agriculture; while both of these are significantly less harmful than indiscriminately purchasing meat on the market.

Vegetarianism and veganism remain powerful protests against modern society's disregard for the interests of other animals. But even among the most sincere defenders of animal rights there is no room for self-righteousness. Though the stomachs of vegetarians may not be graves for dead animals, the purest vegan is still indirectly complicit in hidden forms of slaughter. To use the phrase of one early 19th-century carnivore, apparently innocent vegetarian foods 'are ushered into the world on the spoils of the slain'.

Let us ignore for the moment the lives of microbes and invertebrates. Seasonally ploughing and harvesting crops will mash up a few moles, slice through a burrow of field mice and crush any ground-nesting bird chicks. Far more significant, however, is the creation of the field in the first place: an act that replaces entire ecosystems, along with all their animal inhabitants.

Inevitable as these side-effects of agriculture are, we do have the opportunity to minimise them significantly – and it is here that the argument against meat becomes compelling. In the 18th and 19th centuries, when populations were growing exponentially and the environment was visibly suffering, both vegetarians and carnivores voiced their worry that meat production required more land than that of vegetables. A sustainable approach to food production – as Rousseau, and later Percy Bysshe Shelley, pointed out – had to involve maximising the number of people that could be fed from each unit of cultivated land. Since then, however, commercial meat production has progressed in the opposite direction, by appropriating more and more of the world's available acreage. Between a third and a half of the world's arable harvest is now given over to feed animals. Most of the crop's nutritional content (which could otherwise have gone to feed humans) is thereby effectively converted into faeces, inedible tissue and heat. Much of the destruction of wildlife and the countryside – Britain's hedges and meadows and the 200m hectares of tropical rainforest since the 1960s – has been committed to supply the inefficient demands of the meat and dairy industry.

Combatants in the 'bloodless revolution' against meat-eating have historically had impossibly idealistic aims; but it is still less realistic to believe that we can continue this profligacy indefinitely. The cries of demographers centuries ago are now backed up by the World Health

Organisation and the UN Food and Agriculture Organisation: on an acre of arable crops, they say, enough food can be grown for up to 20 people; use an acre to produce beef and the number drops to just one. It takes an estimated 100,000 litres of precious water to produce a kilogram of beef, compared with 500 litres for a kilogram of potatoes. According to the dramatic figures of Cornell University ecologist David Pimentel, beef requires up to 27 times more energy to produce than plant protein, suggesting that a blindingly simple way of tackling global warming would be to revert to a vegetable-based diet. Climate change is further ratcheted up by a menagerie of 20 billion farm animals exuding plumes of the potent greenhouse gas methane.

Brazil's Amazonian and Cerrado ecosystems, meanwhile, have been devastated by the advance of cattle ranching and, more recently, soya cultivation, 80% of which is used for animal feed. Most people would not like to chew their way through a heap of endangered monkeys, birds, beetles and plants (or people, for that matter): and yet that is effectively what we do when we buy meat without ensuring the provenance of the feed it was fattened on. Until meat is produced in a sensible fashion, vegetarians will continue to occupy the higher moral ground. At the very least, policy-makers and consumers should be thinking of meat-eating in the same way that we have learned to regard fossil fuel consumption: we cannot eliminate it, but we should at least reduce it.

Fortunately, there is meat on the market that evades many of these problems. As human pastoralists discovered 8,000 years ago, raising animals can be an efficient way of harnessing otherwise unusable resources such as grass. Well-managed hill-farming of cattle and sheep with minimal grain-feeding can even contribute positively to local ecologies, such as heathland, where animals keep down bracken, tree saplings and grasses, allowing the rarer habitat of heather to dominate. New farm subsidies will encourage such practices, thus making them more economically viable.

Feeding unused vegetable matter to animals is another way of turning waste into food, rather than food into waste. As a teenager I raised pigs and chickens on surplus collected from the school kitchens, a local baker, and a vegetable market. The resulting pork was – and would be still if new waste legislation can be negotiated – thoroughly good food, and highly amenable to large-scale application. Witness the recently launched business Fareshare 1st, which will divert some of Britain's enormous quantities of surplus food into animal feed. If we could think past the idea that meat is murder, we would see that raising animals in this way actually reduces humanity's heavy ecological footprint.

Heartless though it may seem to some, among the least harmful things to eat are sustainably culled wild animals. In the absence of natural predators, deer populations in parts of Britain have reached such dense numbers that the woodlands they browse fail to regenerate. Rabbits also are in no danger of being wiped out, and the non-native grey squirrel (whose palatability Hugh Fearnley-Whittingstall highlighted by employing its culinary name, the 'flightless partridge'), can be a pest to forestry as well as a threat to red squirrels. Harvesting animals from the wild will never yield the quantity of the modern meat industry: but it will not cause the waste of valuable resources and pollution inherent in that industry either. Local councils in the Highlands are encouraging school canteens to serve 'Bambi-burgers' to absorb the 70,000 red deer culled each year, thus providing children with a local, free-range meat that has a fraction of the fat and cholesterol of beef.

For centuries, hunting for sport has been vilified. But as a method of gathering food, at least hunting brings the consumer and the consumed into closer contact. It may not accord with the Indian doctrine of non-violence that Oswald embraced, but neither is culling animals necessarily representative of th e west's traditionally rapacious attitude to nature. Exchanging a daily feast of ordinary shop meat for more vegetables and an occasional venison steak would be a difficult choice for most; but if we could imaginatively close the distance between ourselves and the world's impoverished people and the environment that suffer as a result of our food choices, it might be possible. It would also be healthier and far tastier. Which is why, along with the wild blackberries and the horseradish I picked and dug from a grassy verge in Somerset, I recently served guests with sausages made from a deer I shot in the preceding days.

How – when I gazed down my rifle-telescope at the exquisite animal grazing in the woods, twitching the flies away with its ears – did I manage to pull the trigger that ended its life? Although I have been culling deer for 13 years, it is still hard. But I did so by contrasting that one direct individual kill with the innumerable less visible victims of arable agriculture, and by remembering that at the last big party I attended there were barbecued prawns – farmed on bulldozed mangroves, fattened on over-exploited fish stocks, transported away from a hungry part of the world and served to an overfed elite. That I pulled the trigger no doubt came as a shock to some. But I hope that even the most dedicated vegetarian can withhold their fury, while hardened carnivores learn, as a matter of urgency, to limit their wanton destruction of the world's ecologies.

⇨ Tristram Stuart's book The Bloodless Revolution: Radical Vegetarians and the Discovery of India is published by HarperCollins.
20 October 2006

We should eat horse meat, says Ramsay

By David Harrison

Gordon Ramsay is to shatter the last taboo of English cuisine by urging the public to eat horse meat.

The controversial chef claims horse meat is tasty and nutritious and should be part of the British diet.

But his call for horses, long revered as farm and racing animals, to be turned into dinner has sparked revulsion among horse lovers, animal welfare campaigners and vegetarians. Even hardened meat eaters and fellow chefs said it was a dish too far.

The celebrity cook found support from some chefs, who said the meat-eating British were too sentimental about horses and hypocritical because they were happy to eat cows, sheep and pigs. But even they doubted whether horse would become popular.

Ramsay reveals his horse meat stance in a new series of The F-word, which starts on Tuesday on Channel 4. The Scottish-born chef admits: 'I've eaten horse', and says that it is healthy, with lots of iron and half the fat of beef and far more Omega 3 essential fatty acids. He describes horse meat as 'slightly gamey' and 'packed with protein'.

For the programme, Ramsay, sends the presenter Janet Street-Porter to France to look at a horse farm and then to Cheltenham racecourse to cook horse on a barbecue and persuade punters to taste it.

She said: 'In a world of mad cows, we should be opening our eyes to new types of red meat. Horse meat is a really good source of protein and one we should take seriously.'

It is not illegal to eat horse meat in Britain and it was, in fact, consumed in some regions until the Thirties.

But Ramsay's one-time protégé Marcus Wareing, the chef patron at Petrus in London, said that he was appalled by the idea of serving horse meat.

'I would never eat horse and I certainly wouldn't serve it in my restaurants,' he said. 'It's not part of our food culture. It's absolutely unthinkable.'

A spokesman for the Vegetarian Society said: 'Most people will find eating horse abhorrent.'

Clarissa Dickson Wright, one of television's Two Fat Ladies, was sympathetic but said horse meat simply wasn't tasty enough to catch on with the public.

'I have no objection to eating horse meat,' she said. 'But if it was good eating there would be more people eating it.'

Jo White, the head of campaigns for the International League for the Protection of Horses, which was consulted by the programme makers, said: 'It is irresponsible to promote horse meat consumption while failing to inform viewers about the appalling abuses of animals in the industry.'

7 May 2007
© Telegraph Group Limited, London 2007

Beastly ingredients - to avoid!

Information from Animal Aid

As a vegetarian, it's simple to avoid eating lumps of meat or fish, but it's not always so easy to spot the hidden extras – the ingredients from dead animals which are added to foods. Lots more ingredients, while not made from dead animals, are pretty dodgy in other ways. Here are some common items to watch out for and avoid!

Animal fat
When 'animal fat' is listed as an ingredient it means 'fat from a dead animal' and not a dairy product, so avoid it. Cakes, biscuits and margarines often contain animal fats and are not suitable for veggies. Suet, lard and dripping are all animal fat – although you can buy vegetarian suet from most supermarkets these days.

Albumen
Made from egg white (almost definitely battery eggs) and used as a food binder.

Cheese
Unless cheese is labelled 'vegetarian' you can assume it contains animal rennet which is taken from dead calves' stomachs. All major super-markets sell vegetarian cheese these days. Beware of processed or ready-prepared foods which contain cheese – unless they have the V symbol, they won't be vegetarian.

E numbers
Additives not suitable for vegetarians include: E120 (cochineal, from insects), E542 (made from animal bones), E631 and (made from meat or fish) and E904 (shellac, from insects).

There are many others that may or may not be made from animals, for example E471.

Eggs

Many biscuits and cakes and other processed foods contain eggs. If they are not labelled 'free-range' or don't have the V symbol, then you can assume they are from battery hens.

Gelling agents

Vegetarians do not eat gelatine or aspic as they are made from dead animals and fish. Veggie alternatives include pectine, agar agar (made from seaweed) and gelozone. You'll need to watch out for gelatine in sweets, jelly and yoghurts, etc.

Lactose

Vegans don't eat lactose because it is made from milk. It is a type of sugar and is commonly used to help flavourings 'stick' to crisps, etc.

Lanolin

You'll see this listed on some cosmetics. It comes from sheep's wool and is usually a slaughterhouse by-product, so most veggies avoid it.

⇨ The above information is re-printed with kind permission from Animal Aid. Visit www.animalaid. org.uk for more information.

© Animal Aid

Vegetarian-friendly supermarkets

Waitrose and Morrisons come top of vegetarian- and vegan-friendly supermarket poll

In August 2006, Animal Aid launched a nationwide survey to find Britain's most vegetarian- and vegan-friendly supermarket chain, monitoring more than 600 supermarkets across the UK. Now we can announce that the winners of the 2007 Animal Aid Vegetarian & Vegan Supermarkets of the Year are Morrisons for its vegetarian provision and Waitrose for its vegan provision. Overall, Waitrose was found to be the most vegetarian and vegan friendly supermarket in Britain owing to its provision of meat- and dairy-free products across the spectrum.

The news comes as Animal Aid launches Veggie Month – a celebration of the benefits of a meat-free diet, which is staged every year throughout March.

Waitrose is renowned for its ethical stance and this latest award follows last year's announcement that it had been named the most farm animal-friendly supermarket chain by Compassion in World Farming. A month later, it was named as the most environmentally-friendly supermarket group in a study by the National Consumer Council.

Says Animal Aid's Vegetarian Campaigner, Kelly Slade:

'The demand for non-animal food products is growing rapidly. Animal Aid's survey shows that, while some supermarkets provide a good range of vegan and especially vegetarian foods, and stock a wide selection of fresh, frozen and chilled products, others have a very long way to go. Animal Aid would like to see supermarkets taking vegetarian and vegan consumers seriously and increasing their provision of chilled and frozen products, especially dairy-free alternatives. This would also be welcomed by a significant proportion of the population who are lactose-intolerant. Our survey showed that labelling is key to reaching target customers and, although the majority of supermarkets have now adopted vegetarian labelling of their own-brand products, most still do not label their vegan products.'

The supermarket branch that scored highest of all 622 stores surveyed was Waitrose in Beaconsfield.

Note

According to a study by the leading market research company, Consumer Analysis Group, six per cent of the population is totally vegetarian and a further 2000 people a week stop eating meat. Already, 40 per cent of the population avoid eating meat at least once a week. Britain has the second largest number of vegetarians in Europe after Germany, with the UK vegetarian food market valued at £700 million per annum in 2006. There is also a rising population of vegans in Britain, currently estimated to be around 250,000.

26 February 2007

⇨ The above information is reprinted with kind permission from Animal Aid. Visit www.animalaid. org.uk for more information.

© Animal Aid

Scientists measure red meat cancer risks

Information from Cancer Research UK

Scientists say that they have identified one of the main links between a diet high in red meat and an increased risk of bowel cancer.

Researchers at the MRC Dunn Human Nutrition Unit and the Open University found that people who eat two or more portions of red meat every day have a significantly higher level of cellular DNA damage than people who ate one portion or less a week.

A study by the same team last year showed that the risks of bowel cancer could be increased by as much as a third among people with high-red meat diets.

Nearly 17,000 currently die from the disease every year in the UK.

'These combined discoveries have allowed us to link red meat consumption to an increased risk of bowel cancer and may give us some clues about developing a screening test for very early changes related to the disease,' said Professor David Shuker, who headed the Open University team.

The study suggested that the increased cancer risk could be caused by substances called N-nitrosocompounds, which form in the large bowel after eating red meat.

These are thought to combine with DNA and make cells more susceptible to changes or mutations which can increase their likelihood of becoming cancerous.

'This study strengthens the link between red meat and bowel cancer by showing that chemicals in red meat can damage DNA,' said Ed Yong, science information officer at Cancer Research UK.

'While it doesn't mean that everyone should go vegetarian, it does emphasise that eating a healthy, balanced diet is very important for reducing your risk of cancer.

'Cancer Research UK's Reduce the Risk campaign advises people to eat lots of fibre, fruit and vegetables, and cut down on red and processed meat.'

⇨ This information is reprinted with kind permission from Cancer Research UK. Visit www.cancerresearchuk.org for more information.

© *Cancer Research UK*

Red meat linked to breast cancer

Information from the University of Leeds

Eating red meat increases a woman's chance of developing breast cancer, according to new research from the University of Leeds.

The findings are most striking for post-menopausal women – those with the highest intake of red meat, the equivalent to one portion a day (more than 57 grams) - run a 56 per cent greater risk of breast cancer than those who eat none. Women who eat the most processed meat, such as bacon, sausages, ham or pies, run a 64 per cent greater risk of breast cancer than those who eat none.

Researchers at the University's Centre for Epidemiology and Biostatistics have been tracking the eating habits and health of more than 35,000 women for the past seven years, and their latest findings are published in the British Journal of Cancer. Earlier findings, widely reported in January, showed that pre-menopausal women who have the greatest intake of fibre have cut their risk of breast cancer in half.

⇨ This information is reprinted with kind permission from the University of Leeds. Visit www.leeds.ac.uk for more information.

© *University of Leeds*

Let's meat up again

Roast pork is back on the menu for ex-vegetarian Rosemary Behan

It was on an island in Cambodia when I finally cracked. The choice between barracuda barbecued in a lemon and pepper sauce and a bread roll was no contest.

Drawn by the mouth-watering smell of the flesh, and faced with the look of amazement on the faces of my hosts when I tried to explain that I had not eaten meat, fish or eggs for 30 years, my long-held belief that vegetarianism was a healthier way of life collapsed.

The physical result was astonishing. It was like a shot of adrenaline: I felt instantly energised and my mind seemed calmer and more focused.

The experience spurred me into trying further dishes all over south-east Asia: beef noodle soup and meaty spring rolls in Vietnam, spicy ginger chicken in Laos, honey-roast pork in China and sushi in Hong Kong. Apart from the pork (delicious), it wasn't the taste that drove me but my sense of wellbeing. My digestion improved, I felt satisfied and lost a stone in six months.

I am not alone. Madonna is probably the most famous celebrity to have quietly returned to eating meat, possibly feeling that such an extreme restriction to her diet might be jeopardising her phenomenal levels of energy and vitality.

Reese Witherspoon, once promoted by the animal rights group PETA (People for the Ethical Treatment of Animals) as one of the 'world's sexiest vegetarians', appeared this year on US television demonstrating her favourite recipe, coq au vin. Asked about the ingredients, she replied: 'Cook it with bacon. Everything tastes better with bacon.'

Drew Barrymore is another former veggie who has adopted a postmodern attitude to ideology, saying: 'I don't eat a ton of meat, and don't wear a ton of leather, but I no longer put strict restrictions on myself.' This view was echoed by the ex-vegetarians I met on my round-the-world-trip, who saw vegetarianism as too austere and uncompromising.

I had previously believed that there were enough alternatives to meat in the form of vegetables, grains and soya. But are these alternatives good enough?

According to David Nicolson, director of the Institute for Optimum Nutrition, the increased energy I noticed when I ate meat may have been because my previous diet was lacking in the protein and fatty acids, particularly the Omega 3 group, that are essential for the production of hormones and the proper functioning of the brain and nervous system.

'Omega 3 fatty acids cannot be manufactured by the body and must be acquired through our diet,' says Nicolson. 'If you are not eating fish, the only way of getting them is by eating walnuts, pumpkin seeds and linseed, which contain alpha-linolenic acid. However, this must then be converted by the body.'

This conversion depends on your levels of B-vitamins and zinc. 'If you are low in those the amount you will be able to produce is minute,' says Nicolson. 'Eating cold-water fish such as salmon, trout, sardines, pilchard or tuna is better because the fish have done the conversion for you.'

My previous diet, with its dependence on cheese and processed soya for protein, and Marmite for vitamin B12, was probably high in saturated and hydrogenated fats and salt, according to Nicolson. 'There are things in meat and meat products, such as iron, which can be much more difficult to get from a vegetarian diet,' he adds.

Dr Frankie Phillips, a spokesperson for the British Dietetic Association, says that it is 'perfectly possible' to eat a balanced diet as a vegetarian, but that it requires more thought and effort. 'The more restrictive your diet is, the more difficult it is to find a balance,' she says.

Tina Fox, the chief executive of the Vegetarian Society, says that between five and 10 per cent of the British population now follow a vegetarian diet, but that numbers are steady. 'I can't imagine anyone ever wanting to go back to eating meat,' she adds.

Personally, I wish I had started a lot sooner.

⇨ *The Institute for Optimum Nutrition (0870 979 1122, www.ion.ac.uk); the British Dietetic Association (0121 200 8080, www.bda.uk.com); the Vegetarian Society (0161 925 2000, www.vegsoc.org).*

Why eat meat?

⇨ It is what dieticians call a 'complete' protein. Meat, fish, poultry, eggs, cheese and milk contain all of the eight essential amino acids needed by the body for growth and development. Soya and quinoa, a South American seed, are the only two vegetarian foods that contain a balance of all eight amino acids.

⇨ Incomplete proteins, which contain only some essential amino acids, are found in grains, legumes and green leafy vegetables, but the correct combination of these foods, such as rice and beans, is required to obtain complete forms of protein from vegetarian diets.

⇨ Meat contains a large number of vitamins and minerals, including those more difficult to obtain from a vegetarian diet, such as vitamins B2 and B12, vitamin D, iron and zinc.

⇨ Meat is a natural food, free of damaging, man-made, hydrogenated fats and oil.

18 September 2006
© *Telegraph Group Limited, London 2007*

Going dairy-free

Information from Animal Aid

Switching from dairy products to cruelty-free alternatives is easier than you'd think. The range of dairy substitutes is growing rapidly and there are now vegan versions of milk, cream, cheese, yoghurt, custard, margarine and many more food products.

What can I use instead of milk?

Soya milk is now widely available. You can buy it in supermarkets and health food shops and it is served in some cafés and restaurants. Soya milk tastes just like cows milk to some people, although others find it has a 'beany' aftertaste.

> ### Switching from dairy products to cruelty-free alternatives is easier than you'd think. The range of dairy substitutes is growing rapidly

There are a variety of different brands available and all taste slightly different. Provamel is the most popular brand. You can buy sweetened, unsweetened, concentrated, organic, long-life, vanilla flavoured and vitamin enriched. Try a range of brands to see which you prefer.

If you find the slightly beany flavour hard to get used to at first try mixing it with a little cow's milk and weaning yourself onto it gradually. Most people find that once they have been using soya milk for a few months, cow's milk is impossible to go back to, as it begins to taste fatty and sour.

As well as soya milk, you can buy rice milk, oat milk, pea milk and almond milk from health food shops. Rice milk has a thinner consistency and sweeter flavour than soya milk

and does not really work in hot drinks, but it is excellent on its own or with breakfast cereals. Oat milk can be used in the same way as soya milk. Pea milk is sold under the brand name White Sun and has an unusual flavour which people have very divided opinions about. Almond milk is a new product which is gaining popularity.

I'll miss cheese too much!

Soya-based cheese alternatives are available from health food shops. The most popular brand is Cheezley, which melts slightly and is therefore good for cooking with. Vegetarian Parmezano is a powdered parmesan substitute, which tastes remarkably like the real thing. Soya cheeses have a similar flavour to Cheddar and Cheshire cheese, but are not quite as sweet or fatty and the texture is quite different, so many people prefer to use them grated.

What about yoghurt?

You can buy soya yoghurts from health food shops and some supermarkets. Yofu and Sojasun are natural yoghurts which come in plastic tubs and taste almost exactly the same as dairy yoghurt. Yofu is also available in fruit flavours, which are very popular. You can also buy several different brands of soya yoghurts in small foil-topped cartons, which come in a variety of flavours.

Is plain chocolate vegan?

Always check the ingredients as many brands contain butterfat or milk powder. To be absolutely sure that a brand is dairy-free, contact the manufacturer or refer to the Vegan Shopper (available in the online shop), because companies often use the same machinery to make milk and plain chocolate and so traces of dairy products can contaminate plain chocolate which is otherwise made to a vegan recipe. Continental plain chocolate is far more likely to be vegan than British brands.

Is vegetable margarine vegan?

Sadly, most of the big brands contain lactose or whey, which are both dairy-derived. However, the range of dairy-free margarines is growing and most supermarkets now stock their own

I'll have the eggs and bacon, with the cheese sauce, and a white coffee.

I will go for the polenta, soy cheese and mushroom omelet, and a soy latte.

Spot the vegan

dairy-free brands. The Pure brand of margarine is stocked in a wide range of shops. Health food shops generally stock several types of vegan margarines and low-fat spreads.

How can I create dairy-free versions of my favourite foods?

Soya milk, tofu, soya cheese, soya yoghurt, coconut milk, ground cashew nuts and yeast flakes can all be used creatively in your favourite recipes in place of milk and cheese.

Custard can be made in the usual way with soya milk or rice milk, or buy a carton of Provamel vanilla soya dessert and use this as custard.

Cheesecake filling can be made by blending together tofu, sugar, vanilla essence and fruit.

Delicious vegan Ice Cream is made by several companies and is hard to distinguish from dairy ice cream. The Swedish Glace brand is particularly good.

Mild curries like sag aloo can be given a creamy texture by cooking with vegetable ghee and adding soya yoghurt or coconut milk.

Milky soups can be made with soya milk and spicy soups can be given a great flavour and texture with coconut milk.

Milkshakes can be made by blending any milk-alternative with syrup, fruit or soya ice cream. You can also buy Provamel OY drinks in chocolate, strawberry and banana flavours from supermarkets and health food shops.

You can even buy dairy-free fudge, nougat, coffee-whitener and pizzas!

Giving up dairy products – action plan

1. Investigate the growing range of dairy alternatives available from shops. Try them to see which brands you like.
2. Try tofu, soya milk and other vegan products in your favourite recipes. Experiment to see what works for you.
3. Invest in some good vegan cookbooks and try some new recipes. You can buy them from Animal Aid (through the online shop), Viva! and Amazon.co.uk. Many high street book shops have a vegetarian and vegan cookery section. Waterstones and Dillons are particularly good.
4. The internet is a brilliant source of advice and recipes.
5. Educate yourself about vegan nutrition. Find out the facts about calcium and osteoporosis, vitamin D and other issues. You can then respond with confidence when concerned friends and relatives accuse you of neglecting your health.
6. Put pressure on your work or college canteen and local catering establishments to provide dairy-free food and drinks for you. Forward them a copy of the Vegan Society's catering pack. Point out that an increasing number of people are going vegan and that many people are allergic to dairy products, so they could tap in to a significant market.
7. Once you have become confident about being vegan, try introducing your friends to dairy-free dishes and discussing the issues with them If they are curious. They might be very receptive.

⇨ The above information is re-printed with kind permission from Animal Aid. Visit www.animalaid.org.uk for more information.

© Animal Aid

Veganism and the issue of protein

Information from PETA

Can the vegan (strict vegetarian) diet provide adequate protein for sound human health? Although the British Nutrition Foundation and the medical community are in scientific

---

Protein is essential to human health

---

unanimity about the health advantages of a vegan diet, the protein question stays with us largely because animal products have been promoted by the industries that produce and sell them as the best source of protein.

This dietary assumption is wrong and can even be harmful, as a quick study of the facts about vegetable protein and nutrition shows.

The importance of protein

Protein is essential to human health. Our bodies – hair, muscles, fingernails and so on – are made up mostly of protein, and it is needed for cell growth and repair. As suggested by the differences between our muscles and fingernails, not all proteins are alike. This is because differing combinations of any number of 20 amino acids may constitute a protein. In much the same way that the 26 letters of our alphabet serve to form

millions of different words, the 20 amino acids serve to from different proteins.

Amino acids are a fundamental part of our diet, and while half of the 20 can be manufactured by the body in one way or another, the other 10 cannot. These 'essential' amino acids (called 'essential' because we must consume them) can easily be provided by a balanced vegan diet.

How much protein?

As babies, our mothers' milk provided the protein we needed to grow healthy and strong. Once we start eating solid foods, non-animal sources can easily provide us with the necessary protein. Only 10 to 15 per cent of the total calories consumed by the average human being need be in the form of protein. People under special circumstances (such

Eating too much animal protein has been directly linked to the formation of kidney stones and has been associated with cancer of the colon and liver

as pregnant women) are advised to get a little more. Vegans should not worry about getting enough protein; if you eat a reasonably varied diet and ingest sufficient calories, you will undoubtedly get enough protein. Protein deficiency, or 'kwashiorkor', is very rare and is usually diagnosed in people living in countries suffering from famine.4

Eating too much animal protein has been directly linked to the formation of kidney stones and has been associated with cancer of the colon and liver. By replacing animal protein with vegetable protein, you can improve your health while enjoying a wide variety of delicious foods.

Vegetarian households in the UK

Food Standards Agency – Consumer Attitudes to Food Standards Survey 2005. UK wide survey of 3,143 householders Sept/Oct 2005.

Households reportedly containing at least one vegetarian member 4%

Non-vegetarian households 96%

Households containing at least one member who ate no meat except fish 5%

Meat-eating households 95%

Figures were 7% among 16-25 year olds and 18% among 26-35 year olds compared to at most 3% among the older age groups. By social group ABs were 7% compared with DEs 3%. Respondents of non-white ethnic origin were 10% compared with white respondents 3%. *Source: FSA. Crown copyright. Quoted by Vegetarian Society: www.vegsoc.org*

Nevertheless, some readers will still wonder, 'But how much protein is in vegan foods?' There's a little sampling for you in the box below.

As this demonstrates, protein deficiency is no more of a concern for vegans than for meat-eaters; if you're getting enough calories, and they're not all from colas and French fries, you'll get enough protein. In fact, if we ate nothing but wheat, oats or potatoes, we would easily have more than enough protein. Eating

nothing but cabbage would provide more than twice as much protein as anyone would ever need!

Of course, a vegan would never be limited to just one food. The vegan diet can (and should) be full of a wide variety of delicious foods. Call 0800 328 9621 for some recipes and cooking tips to get you and your family started.

References

1) The British Nutrition Foundation, 'Protein', 2003.
2) University of Arizona, Department of Biochemistry and Molecular Biophysics, 'Amino Acids Problem Set', The Biology Project, 25 Aug. 2003.
3) World Health Organisation, 'FAO/WHO Launch Expert Report on Diet, Nutrition and Prevention of Chronic Diseases', 23 Apr. 2003.
4) MEDLINEplus Medical Encyclopedia, 'Kwashiorkor', 25 Sep. 2003.
5) Agricultural Research Service, 'Nutrient Data Laboratory', United States Department of Agriculture, 20 Aug. 2003.

⇨ The above information is reprinted with kind permission from PETA. Visit www.peta.org.uk for more information.

© PETA

Percentage of calories from protein (5)

Food	Percentage
Baked beans	21%
Broad beans	31%
Chickpeas	21%
Couscous	13%
Endive	29%
Hummus	19%
Kidney beans	58%
Oats (porridge)	17%
Peanut butter	17%
Peanuts	18%
Pistachio nuts	15%
Pumpkin seeds	18%
Rice (white)	7%
Sesame seeds	12%
Spaghetti (whole wheat)	14%
Tofu	43%
Veggie bacon	14%

(Value per 100 grams edible portion)

Being vegan – a guide

Information from the Vegan Society

You've already taken the first step. The decision to go for it and give up those last few slices of cheese and those oh-so-tempting sponge cakes is the biggest hurdle you'll face, and an easy one at that, because there is a startling array of vegan alternatives that you can find in any wholefood shop and, increasingly, on supermarket shelves.

Within weeks you'll be looking back and wondering what on earth the fuss was about, with the knowledge that a vegan diet is kinder to your health, and kinder to animals, people and the planet.

This guide is here to make it even easier for you to eat and live vegan. If you have any questions that are not answered here, browse our web pages: http://www.vegansociety. com/html/facts/ or contact us at info@vegansociety.com or on 0845 458 8244.

Some common questions

How healthy is a vegan diet?
A well balanced wholefood vegan diet is up there with the healthiest of diets. It can improve your quality of life and decrease your chances of succumbing to many significant diseases, including heart disease, stroke, diabetes and some cancers.
General Guidelines.
If you want a diet that is not just good, but super-healthy, ensure it is varied. Eat plenty of fruit and vegetables, especially those with strong colours, as they tend to have more nutritional benefits. Also include plenty of wholegrains and cut down on processed foods, especially hydrogenated fats. Generally, the more processed a food is, the less nutrients it contains. Ensure you have a reliable source of B12, iodine, selenium, omega 3 and vitamin D2. You may find our multivitamin Veg1 useful. It has been designed specifically for vegans, though it is suitable for everyone.

These are sound guidelines for any diet, whether meat-based, vegetarian or vegan. They are only intended as a brief summary, for more details see our booklet 'Plant Based Nutrition: Healthy Eating Without Animal Products'.

Is it expensive to eat vegan?
That all depends on you. If you go for pricey convenience foods every day it might be costly, but then that would be expensive on any diet. Some products like vegan cheese are more expensive than their animal-derived equivalent but others are cheaper so overall there is no reason why you should have to spend more money. If you prepare most of your meals from basic ingredients and only use pre-packaged convenience foods some of the time, you can eat very cheaply.

What about when I eat out with my friends who eat meat?
Many omnivorous restaurants now cater for vegans, just ask. If they don't, tell them to contact us and we'll vegducate them!

Alternatively, take your friends to a veggie café or restaurant. To find your nearest, check Vegetarian Britain. This extensive guide to vegetarian and vegan eating across Britain is available from The Vegan Society for £9.95 plus p&p.

For a vegan sandwich or snack, go to a health food store. Supermarkets and coffee shop chains are now beginning to cater for vegans as well so are worth checking out.

Make sure you take one of our feedback cards so you can congratulate each food outlet (or not!) on the vegan food they provide.

How do I know a food is vegan?
These days more and more products are marked as vegan which makes life much easier when you are out shopping. To be in the know about the items that aren't marked vegan, equip yourself with a copy of our Animal Free Shopper. This is a pocket-sized guide to all things vegan, from ready meals to suntan lotion, so when you're faced with a huge list of E-numbers or six syllable phenyletho-whatsits, you can just skip to the relevant page, find your product and you're sorted. It costs

just £4.95 plus p&p from The Vegan Society.
How can I replace my favourite foods?
You can replace animal products very easily. From vegan ice-cream to cream cheese and cheatin' meats, there is quite literally nothing that you can't find a vegan replacement for – including those sponge cakes! The section below explains in detail how to go about using the kinder alternatives to animal products.

Not everyone likes the idea of 'substitutes' for animal products – and it's true that they are completely unnecessary in terms of providing all the nutrients your body needs – but they do taste good, and can be especially helpful for new vegans with old cravings.

Instead of...

Chocolate Look out for Organica, who produce a delicious 'milk' chocolate, and a vegan white chocolate. Plamil's range of chocolate, meanwhile, is entirely vegan. Green and Black's do some vegan chocolate and their range is very widely available, check the back of the packet to confirm it is vegan. There are also chocolate truffles, cakes and sweets available, mainly from health

---

There is a startling array of vegan alternatives that you can find in any wholefood shop and, increasingly, on supermarket shelves

---

food shops. You can even get a vegan chocolate easter egg!

Cheese Vegan cheese is now widely available in health food shops. Some of the hard ones do not melt but can be used in sauces, pies, and sandwiches. Recently Redwoods rushed to the rescue of all the die-hard fans of melting cheese and produced several different varieties that don't just melt, they super-melt. They are perfect on pizza and for that old favourite cheese on toast. There are other brands of melting cheese, just check the packet for details.

Vegan cream cheese is also available, while nutritional yeast flakes give a fantastic cheesy flavour and can be used in sauces, lasagne and pizza. Both are available from health food shops.

Milk Soya milk and a whole host of other milks like oat and rice milk can be used to replace cow's milk. Soya milk is the most popular and can be bought from most supermarkets and health food shops. A great introduction to soya milk is the soya milk shakes that are available in

several flavours including chocolate, vanilla, strawberry and banana.

Soya milk also makes excellent cappuccinos and is perfect for making custard, rice puddings and sauces.

Pouring and whipped soya cream is also available, and delicious vegan yogurts and soya desserts. Try soya yoghurt on top of cereals.

Ice Cream Dairy-free ice cream (made from oats or soya) is so good many people will not notice the difference. Just try it and you won't need any further convincing! This is available in some supermarkets like Sainsbury, and practically all health food stores stock it.

Alternatively try luscious light sorbets, these are available in all supermarkets and many are vegan.

Honey There's a whole range of sugars and syrups that can be used as sweeteners. Give maple syrup, agave syrup, date syrup, molasses, dried fruit or fruit jams a try.

Eggs Without eggs, most people want to know how to make a cake. Great cakes can be made without eggs. Some like to use a tablespoon of soya flour in place of each egg or use egg-replacer products (found in most wholefood shops). Try our sumptuous chocolate blueberry cake for an example of a delicious vegan cake.

Even mayonnaise is available without eggs, and it is easy to make vegan quiche and mousse. To replace scrambled egg, try scrambled tofu.

Butter The easy availability of vegan margarines means that butter is easily replaced. In place of animal fats you can use vegetable oil, solid vegetable fat or vegetable suet; and in place of animal stock use vegetable stock or yeast extract. There are also alternatives to gelatine, and vegan jelly crystals can be found in your local health food shop and some supermarkets.

Meat In place of meat there are many cheatin' meats available in health food shops and some supermarkets.

Hamburger There are many different varieties of vegan burgers and sausages available. To accompany them choose from vegan mayo, ketchup, HP sauce, mustard,

sauer-kraut, gherkins, red onions and of course salad.

Mince Use soya mince. Most frozen soya mince is vegan and tastes great in dishes like chilli and shepherd's pie. If you use dried soya mince try soaking it in vegetable stock first. Alternatively try marinated tofu for a more healthy option.

Bacon Vegan Rashers are now available from health food shops.

Treat yourself! As you can see there are a huge variety of vegan treats out there but you may find that you need to slightly change your shopping routine. As well as a few treats in the supermarket you will find many of the compassionate alternatives outlined above in your local health food shop. If you don't have a health food shop nearby it is well worth making a special trip once a week to stock up on foods that are not available in your local shops.

Vegan recipes

The Vegan Society has a great range of vegan recipe books available, contact us for a sales catalogue or look on our website.

⇨ The above information is reprinted with kind permission from the Vegan Society. Visit www.vegansociety.com for more information.

© Vegan Society

Non-dairy cheese substitutes are available in health food shops

Animal sentience

Information from Compassion in World Farming

The basis of all CIWF's work on farm animal welfare is the recognition that animals are sentient beings.

This means they are capable of being aware of sensations and emotions, of feeling pain and suffering, and of experiencing a state of well being. CIWF believes that our own behaviour towards animals should be guided by this recognition of their sentience.

Most of us use animal products every day, but how much do we know about the animals' needs and wants, or about their emotional lives?

Most of us use animal products every day, but how much do we know about the animals' needs and wants, or about their emotional lives?

What is Animal Sentience – and why does it matter?

Humans share the planet with as many as 4700 species of mammals, 9700 species of birds, 4800 species of amphibians, over 23,000 species of fish and around 6000 species of reptiles (as far as we know up to now), not to mention the countless species of invertebrate animals. We interact with and use animals in a multitude of ways in our daily lives.

But how much do we know about how these animals experience the world – what they feel, why they behave in the ways they do, how they understand their environment, how and what they communicate?

Many of us at some time must have watched another animal – a dog, a cat, a horse, a bird, a flock of sheep – and wondered, 'What is she feeling now?' or 'Why is he behaving like that?' or 'What do they want?'. Questions like these may seem simple, even simple-minded, but in fact they are very complex and important to our understanding of the place of humans in the natural world.

Increase in scientific knowledge

A huge increase in scientific research on animal sentience is beginning to answer some of the questions about animal sentience and animal consciousness, although many unsolved mysteries and questions remain for future study and debate. This will be one of the most exciting areas of biology in the coming decades. And the answers have

big implications which are being explored by philosophers and lawyers. How should we treat other animals? What are our responsibilities to them? Do they have rights?

Scientific studies of animal sentience

The most basic way of experiencing the world is through feeling or sensation. 'Sentience' is defined as the ability to have perceptions and sensations. A 'sentient animal' is an animal that is aware of his/her surroundings and of what happens to him/her and is capable of feeling pain and pleasure, at the least. The current scientific consensus is that all vertebrate animals, at least, are capable of feeling pain and experiencing distress. (For this reason anti-cruelty laws exist in many countries.)

But many of the animals we interact with turn out to have more complex mental and emotional lives than people have understood in the past, and new scientific research is constantly revealing new evidence of animals' cognitive abilities and their emotions.

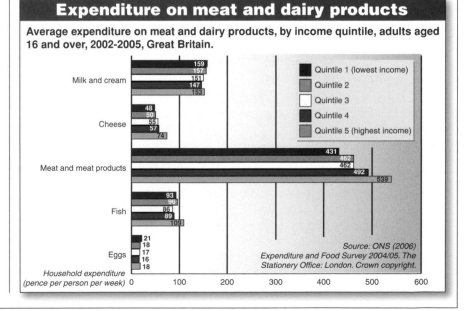

Expenditure on meat and dairy products

Average expenditure on meat and dairy products, by income quintile, adults aged 16 and over, 2002-2005, Great Britain.

Source: ONS (2006) Expenditure and Food Survey 2004/05. The Stationery Office: London. Crown copyright.

Sentient animals have preferences and intentions

It turns out that some animals can both remember and anticipate events and some can foresee their future needs and plan ahead. They can maintain complex social relationships in their groups. Some animals can understand what another animal is going to do, and attempt to deceive that animal in order to gain an advantage. Some animals can enjoy learning a new skill. Some animals react to other animals in ways resembling human empathy. On the negative side, animals can experience the unpleasant emotions of pain, fear, frustration and probably boredom as well. They can be reduced to a state resembling human depression by chronic stress or confinement in a cage.

The facts and theories of animal sentience are still hotly debated among scientists and philosophers

---

All these abilities listed above have been documented in scientific research. Of course these abilities vary between different species. And of course we cannot assume that if an animal behaves in ways that look familiar to us, the animal has the same mental experiences as a human would have in similar circumstances. In the current state of knowledge it is impossible to prove beyond doubt what an animal is feeling, or perhaps thinking. But it is equally important not to underestimate animals' feelings and the sophistication of their mental processes, because this may well affect how we behave towards animals.

Importantly, several of the abilities that have in past been thought to be uniquely human – for example, the use of tools, the ability to plan ahead, the ability to empathise with another or to deceive another, the transmission of skills in ways that can be classified as 'culture', behaviour that can be classified as 'morality' – are now known to exist to some extent among non-human animals too. From the point of view of evolutionary biology, it makes sense that humans should share many of our emotional and cognitive abilities with some of the other animal species.

Understanding animals

Throughout history people have known that animals do very 'clever' and impressive things – such as a bird building an intricate nest or a mother animal teaching her young. Folk stories all over the word attribute intelligence and cunning to animals.

But for much of the 20th century scientists believed that all animal behaviour could be explained either as innate behaviour patterns in response to internal or external stimuli or as conditioned learning in response to stimuli.

Emotion or problem-solving on the part of the animal were not considered necessary to explain its behaviour and it was considered impossible to study these aspects at all. What is exciting about the present time is that scientists are once again interested in studying animals' emotions and mental processes and that huge progress in understanding animals is being made.

Implications of animal sentience

The facts and theories of animal sentience are still hotly debated among scientists and philosophers. But most people have over history assumed that many animals feel pain, hunger, thirst, heat, cold, fear, anger and other basic emotions, because we have everyday evidence that they do.

Why use a whip or stick on a horse unless it feels unpleasant enough to make the horse move faster? If a dog, horse or cow is limping, most people would naturally assume that the animal is in pain. Most people would also assume that the pain is distressing to the animal and, if they could, they would try to do something to alleviate it.

However, throughout history humans have also treated animals in ways that caused great suffering to the animals, whether intentionally or unintentionally. Today there is increasing concern about the welfare of animals, whether these are wild animals or those used by people for food, work, companionship, entertainment, sport or scientific research.

⇨ The above information is reprinted with kind permission from Compassion in World Farming. Visit www.ciwf.org.uk for more information.

© Compassion in World Farming

Free-range eggs and meat: conning consumers?

Information from PETA

In recent years, there has been an increase in the demand for free-range products by a public that is becoming more aware of both the health and moral implications of eating factory-farmed meat and eggs. While free-range products command a high price in supermarkets and delicatessens, and many people are willing to pay for improved conditions on the farms, the reality of 'free-range' farms does not live up to the marketing hype.

Free-range: fact or fiction?

Most consumers believe that the hens who produce 'cage-free' or 'free-range' eggs spend much of their lives outdoors, warming themselves in the afternoon sun, enjoying dust baths and laying their eggs in individual straw nests. But to British egg producers, 'cage-free' and 'free-range' mean something entirely different. 'Cage-free' means only that the animals are not in cages; beyond that, anything goes, and the animals are often crammed inside faeces-ridden sheds, with no ability to engage in any natural behaviours, for their entire lives. 'Free-range' birds also generally spend the majority (if not all) of their lives inside a dark shed with thousands of other birds. These sheds have 'popholes' which allow birds access to the outside and the producers to label their eggs 'free-range'.(1) However, because birds are territorial, the stronger ones monopolise the area around the popholes, while the weaker ones may never cross these territories to get to the exits. These weaker birds may never get outside at all. The areas around the popholes are, not surprisingly, the most desirable areas of the shed, and consequently fights break out amongst the congregated birds. Because aggression, injuries and even cannibalism are rife under these stressful conditions, free-range hens may still be debeaked, a painful practice in which the ends of the birds' sensitive beaks are sliced off.(2)

In their natural environment, chickens can live into their teens and form friendships and social hierarchies.(3) But hens on commercial free-range farms are 'spent' or unable to produce enough eggs to remain profitable within two years.(4) Instead of being allowed to retire, these worn-out hens are usually sold to slaughterhouses, where their bodies are turned into stock cubes, soup or baby food. The hen who laid your 'humane' free-range egg yesterday could easily be shackled upside-down and headed for the scalding tank tomorrow.

Don't be fooled by the label 'free-range' or by Freedom Foods. Birds reared under this scheme do not necessarily have access to the outdoors, either, but instead may spend their entire lives in a shed, rather like a broiler shed, with no fresh air, sunlight or space to carry out their natural behaviours. There is one scheme that does ensure all the birds can walk around outdoors, dust bathe and enjoy the fresh air. That is the Soil Association's scheme, and they stamp their approval on the egg boxes. However, these birds, too, are sent for slaughter after just two years, ending their vastly improved lives in the same terrifying, violent manner.(5)

There is yet another sordid side to this industry, a side that is rarely revealed: the fate of the male chicks. Egg-laying birds must be female. But 50 per cent of the chicks hatched for the egg industry are male, and these financially worthless male birds are slaughtered soon after birth.(6) This is the same for all male chicks, whether they are hatched into the battery, barn or free-range systems.

Organic meat: a product of cruelty

Organic meat, milk and eggs are produced by routinely feeding the animals food that contains no pesticides or antibiotics. Because the animals are often untreated even when sick and because these farms are often quite small and may keep sick and ailing animals around longer, cruelty on such farms can conceivably be worse than on the huge factory farms. The exact definition of organic will depend on which organisation or scheme accredits the particular product, and conditions for the animals can vary greatly. Regardless, all the animals are still rounded up, loaded onto a truck and driven to the slaughterhouse where an agonising death awaits them. Herded in, stunned with an electric current or shot with a captive bolt into the brain, shackled and hoisted up, their throats are slit. They remain upside-down as their failing hearts pump the lifeblood from their bodies. There is no such thing as 'cruelty-free' meat.

'Exotic' animals on the plate

While some people consider it 'adventurous' to eat ostrich burgers, kangaroo fillets or crocodile steaks, many consume non-traditional meats because they believe these animals are reared more humanely than cows, chickens, turkeys or pigs.

Ostriches are native to the hot, dry plains of Africa, where their excellent vision and powerful legs are perfectly suited to the environment. When they are brought to damp and rainy Britain, the birds can run from one side of an average-sized paddock to the other in just a few strides. Skeleto-muscular problems are common as their rapid growth puts tremendous pressure on their bones. This can lead to dislocated joints and fractures, which are caused by chicks' running into obstacles they wouldn't normally come across or losing their footing on the slippery muddy ground. Lameness, loss of appetite, depression and even death can follow. According to the Council of Europe, ostriches succumb more often to disease and have a higher death rate than domesticated farm animals.(7) The only regulations in the UK governing ostrich slaughter are that the animals may not be drowned or suffocated.(8)

The Australian government permits the slaughter of more than 6 million kangaroos a year.(9) While there are laws governing the killing of kangaroos, there are still serious problems with 'weekend hunters', unlicensed shooters who often view kangaroos as 'pests' and have no regard for their suffering. The preferred method of killing joeys whose mothers have been slaughtered is, according to government code, decapitation or a 'heavy blow to destroy the brain'.(10) On their own property, landowners can do whatever they want to kangaroos without fear of repercussions.

In the wild, crocodiles are either shot or captured and taken to overcrowded 'farms'. The females are impregnated and their offspring killed at just 3 years of age. Shooting at point-blank range is the recommended form of slaughter, but where shooting is disregarded for financial reasons, the 'nape stab and pith' method can be used. This involves having workers stand on the head and tail of the crocodile to immobilise him or her; a sharp chisel is then forced between the base of the skull and the first vertebra. When the animal has been stunned, a rod of about 3mm in diameter is used to probe and destroy the brain. In one PETA investigation, slaughter of alligators by bludgeoning them and stabbing them to death was caught on film.

The unhealthy option

Whether it's 'exotic', 'organic' or 'free-range', meat is completely devoid of fibre and contains high levels of saturated fat and cholesterol that are associated with hypertension, stroke and heart disease. Meat is still linked to cancer, kidney stones, osteoporosis and a whole host of other conditions, diseases and illnesses.

The same is true of 'free-range' eggs. They have no fibre, and the cholesterol in them contributes to the furring of the arteries and premature death by stroke or heart attack.

Doing the humane thing

From the 'free-range' hen who smells fresh air for the first time only on her way to the slaughterhouse to the 'humanely-reared' dairy cow whose day-old male baby is taken from her and sold to veal farmers, all animals raised for food suffer and are exploited. The only truly humane alternative to this suffering is to choose alternatives to eggs, milk and meat.

References

1) Alice Hart-Davis, 'Is Any Chicken Safe to Eat?' Evening Standard, 19 Nov. 2002.
2) Lord Beaumont of Whitley, address to United Kingdom Parliament, 21 Jun. 2002.
3) Molly Snyder Edler, 'Chicken Love Leads to Book Deal', OnMilwaukee.com, 26 Sep. 2002.
4) Jacqueline Wepruk, 'The Disposal of Spent Laying Hens', Work & Achievements, Animal Welfare Foundation of Canada, 27 Aug. 2003.
5) Anthony Browne, 'Ten Weeks to Live', The Observer, 10 Mar. 2002.
6) Ibid.
7) Standing Committee of the European Convention for the Protection of Animals Kept for Farming Purposes, 'Recommendation Concerning Ratites', Council of Europe, 22 Apr. 1997.
8) Standing Committee of the European Convention for the Protection of Animals Kept for Farming Purposes.
9) Environment Australia, 'Commercial Kangaroo Harvest Quotas – 2003', 2003.
10) Department for Environment and Heritage, 'The Macropod Conservation and Management Plan for South Australia', Nov. 2002, p. 43.

⇨ The above information is re-printed with kind permission from PETA. Visit www.peta.org.uk for more information.

© PETA

Ethical shoppers

Survey says shoppers would dump usual supermarket for higher animal welfare

56 per cent of people in the UK would dump their usual supermarket in search of higher animal welfare products says a new Eurobarometer survey.

---

56 per cent of people in the UK would dump their usual supermarket in search of higher animal welfare products

---

Compassion in World Farming (CIWF), a leading farm animal welfare organisation welcomes the findings which show that 68 per cent of UK citizens think that farm animal welfare needs improving.

The Eurobarometer Attitudes of EU citizens towards Animal Welfare launched today Thursday 22 March confirms growing demand for companies to take farm animal welfare seriously.

'The new EU survey shows that the European public are so concerned about farm animal welfare that 62 per cent of Europeans (56 in the UK) would change their usual place of shop,' comments Peter Stevenson, CIWF's Chief Policy Advisor who was invited as a special observer to a conference today in Brussels launching the findings.

Initiatives such as CIWF's Compassionate Supermarket of the Year now in its sixth year, and this week's Good Egg Awards, which rewarded among others Sainsbury's, J D Wetherspoon and Starbucks for switching to ethical egg supplies, bring together two unlikely allies – animal welfare campaigners and profit-making food suppliers.

'Its great to see the results of this survey backing up the work we are doing with supermarkets,' says Peter Stevenson, Chief Policy Advisor for Compassion in World Farming who was invited as a special observer to a conference today in Brussels launching the findings.

'We have worked tirelessly with them and food suppliers across the UK and Europe to raise the standards of animal welfare. Now there's even more evidence to show why they need to act. It makes business sense.

'We will keep pushing supermarkets and the food industry to keep raising the standards of farm animal welfare and respond to the public's demands,' concludes Mr Stevenson.
23 March 2007

⇨ The above information is re-printed with kind permission from Compassion in World Farming. Visit www.ciwf.co.uk for more information.

© Compassion in World Farming

A humanist discussion of animal welfare

Information from the British Humanist Association

Most reasonable people think that we ought to treat other people well, that we should respect their rights and consider their welfare. But should we also treat other animals well, and why should we? Do they, too, have rights that we should respect?

Humanists seek to live good lives without religious or superstitious beliefs. They use reason, experience and respect for others when thinking about moral issues, not obedience to dogmatic rules. Humanists have no 'party line' on animal welfare, and no compulsory customs or religious food taboos that would influence their attitude to or treatment of animals.

They have to think for themselves, and decide whether to extend their concern for welfare from humans to animals. Humanists tend to put the needs of human beings first if there is a conflict, and to value animals and the natural world for human-centred reasons. But a rational non-religious morality, based on observation, experience and empathy, is likely to include an unwillingness to cause animals suffering, based on what we know about animal psychology and a respect and affection for animals.

Different cultures, different views

The debate about how we treat animals has gone on a long time, and some cultures see no reason to treat animals well. Religious beliefs that humankind is special and that animals do not have souls have sometimes been used to justify appalling exploitation and cruelty. But religious statements about other species tend to depend on the more general moral values of society and to change as we learn more about animal psychology. Some religious people think that God created the world and gave humans 'stewardship' over it, or look to sacred text for guidance about how to treat animals – but humanists look elsewhere for reasons for caring about animals.

What have scientists and philosophers thought?

Scientists and philosophers have long argued about animal consciousness and suffering. In the 16th century Michel de Montaigne thought that animals were probably very like us: 'Why should we think that they have inner natural instincts different from anything we experience in ourselves?' But in the 17th century, some people, for example the philosopher René Descartes, thought that animals could not feel pain and so we could do whatever we liked to them. A century later, the Scottish atheist philosopher David Hume wrote: 'We should be bound by the laws of humanity to give gentle usage to these creatures', which is probably a common view amongst humanists today. In 1789 the utilitarian Jeremy Bentham wrote of animals: 'The question is not, Can they reason? nor Can they talk? but Can they suffer?' Also in the 19th century, Charles Darwin's theory of evolution taught us how closely related to other animals we are, and how like us they can be. In the 20th century ecologists reminded us of the interdependence of species and the importance of conservation. People also first began to talk of 'animal rights' and 'speciesism', ideas pioneered by the atheist philosopher Peter Singer and still controversial; many people think that rights must be linked with with duties and reciprocity, and it is difficult to see how animals can have duties or respect human rights.

Can animals suffer?

But whether animals can be said to have rights or not, concern for suffering does seem to be the key issue. We do not, on the whole, think it is possible to be cruel to plants because plants do not have nervous systems which can feel physical pain, or minds which can feel psychological pain (for example, fear). But we have all seen miserable or frightened animals or heard them yelp with pain – it is difficult to believe seriously that they do not have feelings, and scientists have confirmed these everyday observations by methodical research. It is hard to be sure about the feelings of animals, but animal welfare scientists are beginning to work out more precisely what animals feel and what causes suffering. Research into the brains of animals shows that their brains and mental states are quite like ours and a great deal of testing on animals is done because we assume they are like us, physically and psychologically. But the more like us they are, the more they can suffer like us and the more they deserve our concern and respect.

Whether animals can be said to have rights or not, concern for suffering does seem to be the key issue

---

What do humanists think?

Humanists would prefer not to cause unnecessary suffering to sentient beings, and discussion tends to focus on what is 'unnecessary suffering' and which animals are sentient. Most people think that fur coats are unnecessary luxuries and that the cruelty involved in farming or hunting animals for their fur cannot be justified. Many people also think that hunting and fishing for food or sport are cruel and unnecessary. Many people are willing to eat less meat, or no meat at all, in order to discourage what they see as the unnecessary cruelty involved in factory farming. (In Europe and the USA, 18 million pigs – intelligent animals – are kept in restrictive battery farm conditions.) Some people think that all killing of animals is wrong, whilst others argue that death cannot mean as much to animals as it does to us, so all that matters is rearing and killing them humanely. Humanists will not think that traditional religious ritual slaughter (where, unlike most of the meat we eat, animals are bled to death without pre-stunning, which evidence shows does cause suffering) should take precedence over killing animals humanely.

Some people oppose using animals for our entertainment, in zoos and circuses, or as pets (sometimes bred for characteristics that make life very difficult for the animal, for example flat faces that interfere with breathing). Humanists make use of reason and compassion when thinking about these questions, and will arrive at different conclusions, often depending on specific circumstances or situations.

The sharpest divisions of opinion amongst humanists (and others) are over the use of animals in experiments. Most people, whatever their worldview, would probably agree that there are enough cosmetics and shampoos in the world to make the testing of new ones on animals unnecessary. But medical research is a different matter. Most of us would not want to use untested drugs or treatments, or to have new medicines tested on ourselves or other people. Many effective medicines and treatments have been discovered and refined in tests on animals, and many humanists would accept these tests as long as the benefits outweigh the costs – though this is not an easy calculation to make. It is also worth

remembering that some research involving animals is intended to improve animal welfare – for example, animals need medicines too. But it is certainly right to ensure that animal experiments are kept to a minimum and conducted as humanely as possible.

The debate about how we treat animals has gone on a long time, and some cultures see no reason to treat animals well

---

Most responsible human beings, and that includes humanists, do not think that we should exploit or mistreat others just because they are different from us or we are bigger or cleverer than they are. Is this what we are doing when we mistreat animals? Most humanists simply do not want to be the kind of person who causes suffering or who tolerates cruelty, and for many that must include animals.

Questions to think about:

⇨ Is the life or pain of a human being worth more than the life or pain of a rabbit? Two rabbits? Fifty rabbits? A thousand rabbits?

⇨ A rabbit is born and lives its whole life in a small barren cage. Does it make any difference to your moral views on this if it is kept (a) as a pet, (b) for meat, (c) for fur, (d) for medical experiments, (e) for beauty product experiments.

⇨ Do you think that animals have a different attitude to death from humans?

⇨ New-born babies could be said to be less sentient, less aware of themselves and others and the past and the future, than adult chimpanzees. Does that mean we should experiment on new-born babies rather than chimpanzees?

⇨ How consistent are you in your ideas about animal welfare? Do you tolerate some uses of animals and not others? Do you kill wasps and flies? Do you eat factory-farmed meat or chicken? Do you avoid thinking about where your food comes from? Should we all be vegetarians? Do you think there should be some kind of sliding scale of concern?

⇨ Some ritually slaughtered meat is sold in butchers, supermarkets, canteens and Indian restaurants without being labelled. Do you think it should be sold or served at all? or just to the religious groups that require it? Do you think it should be clearly labelled? Would you buy or eat it?

⇨ What new issues of animal welfare (if any) does genetic modification raise? Is it right to genetically modify animals for organ donation to humans? Would there be anything wrong in, say, genetically modifying pigs so that they liked being kept in battery pens?

⇨ How are you deciding your answers to these questions? What principles and arguments influence your answers?

⇨ How is the humanist view on this issue similar to that of other worldviews you have come across? How is it different?

With thanks to Dr Georgia Mason of Oxford University Department of Zoology

⇨ The above information is re-printed with kind permission from the British Humanist Association. Visit www.humanism.org.uk for more information.

© British Humanist Association

Eat for animal welfare

If you care about animals, these shopping tips from the RSPCA will ensure your food purhases protect their welfare

⇨ Look for free-range, organic or Freedom Food logos to support higher welfare for animals;

⇨ Familiarise yourself with food assurance scheme logos, what they mean and which ones you'd choose to support. Look for these when you're shopping and vote with your shopping basket;

⇨ Try to buy food produced locally. This is good for the environment, the local economy and, where animals are concerned, this can mean they have not had to travel long distances in production or to slaughter;

⇨ If you can't always buy local, show your support for the British farmer and buy British. There are a series of standards set in place for British food production, through a combination of government legislation and national food assurance schemes, which at least cover minimum welfare standards for animals. It is not as easy to regulate production methods for imported food, so adequate welfare for animals produced outside the UK is much more difficult to assess;

⇨ Take a look at ingredients on the food you buy. All eggs should now be labelled with their method of production, i.e. free-range or eggs from hens kept in battery cages. Some ready-made meals, including some vegetarian ranges, use battery eggs. If the packaging does not detail the production method of the ingredients, you could ask your supermarket or write to the manufacturer to find out;

⇨ If you're not certain that the food you want to buy is produced with animal welfare concerns in mind, ask your supermarket. It should know where the food has come from and how it was produced. Just asking will help raise awareness that consumers are concerned about these issues – make your voice heard.

Information provided by the RSPCA.

⇨ The above information is reprinted with kind permission from TheSite.org. Visit www.thesite.org for more information.

© TheSite.org

Freedom food

Information from the RSPCA

What the Freedom Food mark means

The Freedom Food mark seen on eggs, dairy, meat, poultry and salmon products means the animals involved have been reared, handled, transported and slaughtered to high standards devised and monitored by the RSPCA.

The standards apply to both indoor and outdoor farming methods, as long as they meet the requirements. Freedom Food has demonstrated that high welfare standards can be achieved within commercial farming operations.

Thumbs up

⇨ Freedom Food is entirely independent from the food industry, is non-profit making and exists solely to improve farm animal welfare.

⇨ For egg production, the welfare standards prohibit the use of battery cages for hens. The RSPCA considers that battery cages have inherent animal welfare problems.

⇨ All standards laid out in the Freedom Food assurance scheme are actual requirements, not recommendations. If producers do not meet these requirements their Freedom Food membership will be cancelled.

Thumbs down

⇨ There is no independent consumer input into the process of developing the welfare standards. The Food Standards Agency suggested that: 'a consumer addition could bring wider understanding of consumer aspirations.'

The Freedom Food mark seen on eggs, dairy, meat, poultry and salmon products means the animals involved have been reared, handled, transported and slaughtered to high standards

---

Who set up the scheme?

Freedom Food was set up in 1994 by the RSPCA as the first farm assurance scheme to concentrate primarily on animal welfare. The RSPCA's farm animal department sets the welfare standards for each of the species covered – beef, dairy cattle, sheep, pigs, laying hens, chickens, turkeys, ducks and salmon.

How often are the producers assessed?

For a product to bear the Freedom Food logo, the entire supply chain is assessed. Once part of the scheme, all members have yearly reassessments with a minimum of 30 per cent of farms approved by Freedom Food having additional random spot checks to make sure standards are maintained.

Certification Mark

⇨ The above information is reprinted with kind permission from the RSPCA. Visit www.rspca.org.uk for more information.

© RSPCA

Animal welfare on organic farms

This information sheet aims to answer some general questions about animal welfare on organic farms

What does the Soil Association mean by animal welfare?

The health and well being of animals is central to organic principles. Health should be defined as a positive physical and mental state whereby the livestock are robust and able to resist diseases.

Aspects of animal welfare are enshrined in all organic livestock standards

---

Positive animal welfare means the satisfaction of 'all the animals' needs, including their behavioural needs, not just the avoidance of cruelty. The foundation stones of animal welfare are good nutrition, careful management and the use of appropriate breeds.

Are regulations regarding animal welfare part of all EU organic standards?

Yes. Aspects of animal welfare are enshrined in all organic livestock standards. Organic farming is the only farming system in the EU defined by regulation. (Regulation 2092/92). The regulation lays down minimum rules for organic livestock production. For example, livestock must have access to the outdoors and the number of animals per unit area must be limited. Medicinal inputs and feed supplements are restricted and much of the food that the farm animals eat must be provided on the farm itself.

A division of DEFRA, interpret the EU regulations and set the standards which govern organic production in the UK. These

standards are the legal minimum to which certification bodies in the UK must certify organic foods.

Do all organic certifiers have the same animal welfare standards?

No. All organic certification bodies have to meet the minimum requirement but some bodies, like the Soil Association exceed the minimum in a number of areas. The Soil Association's livestock standards are very detailed and run to over 80 pages compared to the basic UK standards which comprise of about four. The castration of pigs, for example, is not allowed under the Soil Association standards, whereas the EU and basic UK standards do permit this practice.

Are antibiotics allowed on organic farms?

Organic farming is an holistic method of agriculture. Through a positive management approach

to health and welfare, farmers always aim to prevent disease from occurring on the farm. However, if a disease did occur then organic farmers are encouraged to use natural and complementary therapies. But if these are not appropriate then conventional medicines, including antibiotics, must be used. The important thing is that the welfare of the animal is paramount: in other words, if an animal is sick it must be treated.

However the routine or preventative use of antibiotics is prohibited. This is because routine drug use weakens an animal's immune system and so increases the reliance on drugs. When any animal is given antibiotics, its meat or milk cannot be sold for human consumption for a specified period – the 'withdrawal period'. If an organic animal is given antibiotics then the withdrawal period has to be at least doubled and often tripled before the meat or milk can be sold as organic.

Are vaccinations used on organic farms?

Organic farmers aim to build up natural immunity in their livestock to diseases that may be present on their farms. But vaccines can only be used where there is a known disease risk on the farm – or a neighbouring

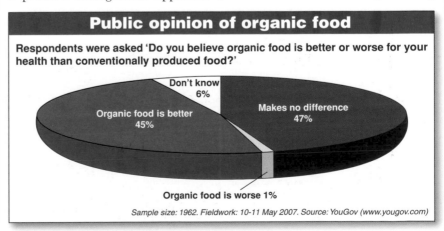

Public opinion of organic food

Respondents were asked 'Do you believe organic food is better or worse for your health than conventionally produced food?'

- Don't know 6%
- Makes no difference 47%
- Organic food is better 45%
- Organic food is worse 1%

Sample size: 1962. Fieldwork: 10-11 May 2007. Source: YouGov (www.yougov.com)

farm – which cannot be controlled by any other means. The farmer needs to provide details of their vaccination strategy in their animal health plan. All organic farms must have an animal health plan which is reviewed annually. This has to be approved by the certification body, it provides an outline of the strategies the farm will adopt to diagnose and remedy any health and welfare problems. Single targeted vaccines are preferred unless there is a problem with multiple diseases.

How do organic farmers prevent their animals from falling ill?

⇨ Building natural vitality and disease resistance.

This may be done by providing a nutritious diet – on most fully organic farms the vast majority of the feed is fully organic. Rotating the pastures on which the animals graze and allowing young animals to develop a natural immunity from their mothers can also help.

⇨ Minimising stress through good management techniques.

Providing good housing – animals must be provided with adequate bedding in lying areas and these areas should consist of solid floors rather than slatted floors which can cause foot problem.

Practising mixed or clean grazing. Often internal parasites are species specific so in order to keep them under control farmers may employ mixed grazing practices. This is where, for example, cattle would graze a pasture one year followed by sheep graze the next.

Alternatively organic farmers may practice clean grazing to break the parasite cycle. This is where the livestock are moved after a set amount of time to land that has not had that kind of livestock on it for several years. For example with pigs, a piece of land would be used by pigs for a maximum of six months and then kept free of pigs for at least four years. This practice is especially important on organic pig and poultry farms

⇨ Selecting breeds which are adapted to local conditions and able to resist disease.

On organic farms, the characteristics of many native breeds play an important role in ensuring the positive health of the animals. They include suitability to locality (climate, elevation and soils), hardiness, thriftiness, disease resistance, a quiet temperament, maternal instinct, and ability to thrive on a high roughage diet.

In the most intensive systems, breeds are used which tend to be faster growing and as well as producing more milk or meat. As a result the welfare of some breeds has been seriously compromised. This can put animals under excessive stress, weaken their natural immune systems and increase reliance on veterinary medicines.

10 April 2006

⇨ The above information is reprinted with kind permission from the Soil Association. Visit www.soilassociation.org for more information.

'Only intensive farming' will feed Britain

⇨ *Organic agriculture 'will never meet demand'*
⇨ *Professor warns of soaring prices and shortages*

Britain must continue to intensify its farming practices to meet soaring demand for cheap food and prevent shortages, a leading agricultural expert said yesterday. Demand for biofuels, booming economies of developing countries and climate change will put demand on food supplies that can only be met by intensive techniques, said Professor Bill McKelvey, head of the Scottish Agricultural College. Prices could soar and future generations in the UK may find they can no longer take plentiful food for granted.

At a London briefing, Prof McKelvey defended intensive techniques and said alternatives such as organic farming would not cope with predicted growth in population.

By David Adam, environment correspondent

'There is a need to continue to intensify farming. Organic farming has a place but it will never feed the growing population of the world,' he said.

Media criticism of modern farming techniques after the bird flu outbreak at the Bernard Matthews turkey farm in Suffolk had been unfair, he said, adding that intensive farming protects the environment because it reduces the amount of land used for agriculture. Europe would also have to overcome its 'illogical' opposition to genetically modified crops to help boost yields, he said.

'In the UK, we are becoming less self-sufficient in food. I think it's possible in the next 25 to 50 years that there will be food shortages in the UK.' The proportion of average British family income spent on food might double from 10% to 20%, he said. The UK currently provides 60% of its own food, and imports were increasing, said Prof McKelvey, who advises industry and the government.

With world population forecast to grow from 6bn to 8.5bn in 50 years, he warned that countries such as New Zealand that export food to Britain were likely to switch attention to China and India. Food demand there is increasing sharply and meat consumption in China has doubled in the last decade. Prof McKelvey said the solution was farmers producing more food on the same amount of land. Wheat production increased four-fold in the last 50 years and in the next 50 years would probably have to rise by the same level again, despite a shortage of suitable land. 'There are only two ways to do that. We either take land from rain forests or we intensify existing farms. We will protect the wild environment by making better use of farms.'

Plant breeding – conventional and using genetic modification – was the best way to produce more food from the same amount of land. Although very little is grown commercially in Europe, millions of hectares of GM crops have been grown across the world in recent years.

'Europe is going to have to face up to using GM crops,' he said. Climate change is also expected to put pressure on food supplies, despite an initial boost in productivity for some crops.

Prof McKelvey said great swathes of agricultural land would be lost to desert, with the effects already felt in areas such as southern Spain. Bio-fuels, a suggested solution to global warming, could bring added problems for food production.

Patrick Holden of the Soil Association, which promotes organic farming, said 'business as usual' intensive farming would not be possible in future because of the fossil fuel costs and the greenhouse gas emissions associated with nitrogen fertilisers. Organic farming could equal and sometimes even exceed the yields of chemical intensive farming systems. 'The challenge that global agriculture confronts today is to research and develop these systems, because we are on the threshold of a post-fossil fuel era.'
18 April 2007

Sunny side up for sales of ethically-positioned eggs

Information from Mintel

Today, more British consumers than ever before are enjoying their full English breakfasts with a clear conscience. Latest research from MINTEL finds the popularity of cheap battery eggs starting to crack, as consumers scramble for ever more boxes of free-range, barn and organic eggs. With their own health as well as that of the chicken in mind, consumers bought some 2.04 billion free range, barn and organic eggs last year, up from just 1.64 billion in 2002 – an impressive 24% increase. Sales of free range eggs in particular have really started to boil over, rising some 31% since 2002 alone.

Although last year battery or laying cage eggs accounted for almost 6 in 10 eggs sold (59%), volume sales of these less welfare friendly eggs fell 8% from 3.19 billion to 2.93 billion between 2002 and 2005.

'The widespread uptake of ethically-positioned eggs by both retailers and consumers is testament to the emotive nature of this particular market. People are becoming increasingly concerned about the way animals are reared and more aware of how environment can impact on the flavour of the food. As such consumers are increasingly turning their backs on eggs from laying cage hens, which are often housed in poor conditions. In turn they have embraced free-range eggs from hens living in more agreeable surroundings, while organic eggs are seen as healthier, as the hens do not come into contact with chemical fertilizers, pesticides, or hormones. When it comes to buying eggs, as well as improved taste, British consumers are clearly looking for choices that are better for their own health, while not compromising that of the chicken,' comments Claire Birks, senior market analyst at MINTEL.

Long live the great British fry-up

Despite busy lifestyles we still find time for eggs in the morning. Breakfast is one of the key occasions when people eat eggs, with over half (52%) of British adults indulging,

whether it be scrambled or poached, fried or boiled.

'The traditional English breakfast has a universal appeal. This is a meal that is served all day, across a wide variety of eating establishments from truckers' cafés to the most exclusive hotels. It is both representative of a working class staple, and a luxury weekend retreat, and is perhaps the only recipe that transcends both the age and gender divide,' comments Claire Birks.

Cracking good sales

Last year spend on all types of eggs hit half a billion pounds (£514 million) for the first time ever, with Brits clearly developing a taste for larger eggs as the combined share of

volume accounted for by large and very large eggs increased from 38% in 2003 to 43% in 2005.

This year, Brits are set to spend £526 million on eggs, up 28% on 2001 figures. What is more, volume sales are expected to smash through the 5 billion egg mark by the end of the year. This equates to an impressive 90 eggs a year for every man, woman and child in the UK today – almost two a week.

'Value growth has outpaced volume as consumers have traded up to more expensive barn, free range and organic eggs, as well as buying larger sizes. But this trend has been tempered by intense price competition between the leading retailers, in a market dominated by

own label brands,' explained Claire Birks.

MINTEL forecasts that the UK egg market will grow by an estimated 17% to reach £617 million over the period 2006-11. With the imminent launch of the black Lion Quality logo – revealed on the egg once boiled properly – hopefully the billions of eggs sold in coming years will be cooked to perfection!

⇨ The above information is reprinted with kind permission from Mintel. Visit www.mintel.com for more information.

© Mintel

The price of eggs

Supermarkets are starting to ban battery eggs from their shelves. But will the alternatives really mean happier hens? Hattie Ellis investigates

Sainsbury's has recently announced that it is to phase out the 150m battery eggs it sells a year. Commendable as this is, cynical people might say that Sainsbury's is bowing to the inevitable. Battery egg production in this country will be illegal by 2012, when a Europewide ban is due to come into force. Still, Sainsbury's is going beyond the legal minimum by also not using eggs from 'enriched' cages, which will be allowed. Just a

step up from the battery, these are unacceptable to welfare campaigners such as Compassion in World Farming (CIWF).

Other supermarkets have already gone further. Marks and Spencer took battery eggs off the shelves nearly five years ago and its ban includes the eggs used in all its other products, not just those sold in the shell. Waitrose has had a free-range policy on its whole eggs since 2001, and uses them in its fresh and chilled food, and some of

its grocery goods, such as pasta. The Co-op has also taken the pledge on its fresh eggs, and is 'working towards' replacing caged eggs with free-range and organic in own-label products.

Consumers, meanwhile, have already chosen. Around 40% of eggs sold fresh are now free-range. But as battery cages are banned, questions have been raised about the supposedly kinder systems that will replace them.

The alternatives are barn eggs, where the birds are kept loose but inside sheds; free-range, where they have access – at least in theory – to the outdoors; and organic, which is free-range with additional requirements such as non-GM feed and smaller flock sizes.

But are we really paying for happier hens? For a start, there is fraud. As demand outstrips domestic supply, more eggs are imported (around a fifth of all the eggs we eat). Defra recently reported on the racket of repackaging imported battery eggs. As many as 500m may have been falsely sold as free-range.

There are concerns, too, about how much the hens really range. Regulations allow free-range flocks to be up to 16,000, though these have

to be subdivided within the shed to groups of 4,000. Locals campaigning against the building of giant sheds by one large producer say they see only a few hundred birds outside one such existing building, even on sunny days.

It is not enough to have the odd pop-hole in the side of a shed, even if this ticks a box on a certification scheme. Chickens need to be encouraged to go outside as they hate open spaces, preferring cover from trees and hedges. Sainsbury's plans to plant trees to produce 'Woodland' free-range eggs and other egg producers have already moved this way.

Battery egg production in this country will be illegal by 2012, when a Europewide ban is due to come into force

---

And free-range systems do not eliminate other welfare issues. In crowded conditions, chickens can be aggressive; feather-pecking and even cannibalism can be rife. To counter this, many free-range birds, as well as battery ones, have the end of their beaks removed. Although technology has improved since the days when a third or even a half of the beak was cut off, animal-welfare campaigners still feel it is wrong, though admittedly better than the hens pecking each other to death.

In Switzerland, where battery cages and beak tipping were both banned in 1991, they manage to have flocks that range without aggression. Stocking density and good farming can do much to solve the problem. 'Let's remember that these are animals and manage our farms as biological systems, not technological systems,' says Dr Michael Appleby, a chicken expert and welfare policy adviser to the World Society for the Protection of Animals (WSPA).

'Birds don't have hands, so how do they manipulate and investigate? With their beaks. The tip is very sensitive,' he says.

Some of the highest standards for egg production are those of the

How many veggies internationally?

Country	% veggies	Inhabitants
Australia	2% (estimate)	20,385,903
Austria	3%	8.1 million
Belgium	2%	10.2 million
Canada	4% (estimate)	31.9 million
Croatia	3.7%	4.5 million
Czech Republic	1-2%	10.2 million
Denmark	1-2%	5.4 million
France	less than 2%	60 million
Germany	9% (survey)	82 million
India	40%	997.5 million
Ireland	around 6% (estimate)	3.7 million
Israel	8.5%	7 million

Country	% veggies	Inhabitants
Italy	10%	57 million
Norway	2%	4.6 million
Poland	under 1%	38.6 million
Portugal	approx 2% (estimate)	10 million
Romania	approx 4%	21.7 million
Slovakia	approx 1%	5.4 million
Spain	approx 4%	40.5 million
Sweden	3 % (estimate)	9 million
Switzerland	3%	7.3 million
The Netherlands	4.3%	16.3 million
UK	9% (high in young people)	59.6 million
USA	4%	265.9 million

Summarised by the European Vegetarian Union.
Figures from different sources: visit www.euroveg.eu/lang/en/info/howmany.php to view.

Soil Association (SA), which is opposed to routine beak trimming. Birds should be kept in flocks of just 500, it says, although they can go up to 2,000 if conditions are good enough. All this makes a difference to the price. Only 3% of eggs sold are organic, and only 7% of these are SA-accredited. Waitrose is the only major supermarket chain to sell SA eggs.

People will pay more, however, for non-organic eggs with more visible selling points. One example is the boom in Clarence Court eggs. The Cotswold Legbar eggs come in cute pastel shades and Burford Browns in chocolatey hues. Such traditional breeds have hardier characteristics that can make them more suitable to the free-range life than the modern hybrid egg machines used in most laying flocks. Kept in flocks of up to 4,000, they lay around 200 eggs a year, as opposed to nearly one daily. They do not need beak trimming. Despite a price tag of around £1.59 for six (standard free-range eggs cost 99p), sales have doubled in the past year and they are widely available in supermarkets.

In the same price bracket come Columbus eggs. The birds are fed on seeds rich in healthy Omega-3 fatty acids and the company claims two eggs a day can give you more than half the recommended daily amount. The British Heart Foundation says these benefits have not been quantified, and recommend eating oily fish. The

British Nutrition Foundation agrees but adds that for those who don't eat fish, fortified foods can be a useful alternative. Not all Columbus hens, however, are free-range.

Even as we move towards higher-welfare eggs, the industry is lobbying hard to get the battery-cage ban postponed, arguing that as conditions improve in Europe, cheaper imports from further afield will take their place. Eggs from beyond the EU do not have the same labelling regulations, and many are sold powdered or as liquid that goes anonymously into processed foods.

And while Sainsbury's and others have made a step in the right direction with eggs, what about the chickens reared for meat? There are around 30m laying birds in Britain and 860m a year raised for meat. Only around 4% of those are free-range.
⇨ Hattie Ellis is the author of Planet Chicken: the shameful story of the bird on your plate (Sceptre, £14.99). To order a copy with free UK p&p go to guardian.co.uk/bookshop or call 0870 836 0875.
18 April 2007
© Guardian Newspapers Limited 2007

⇨ In the last ten years, the number of vegetarians in the UK has more than doubled; there are currently about four million vegetarians in the UK – 7% of the adult population and 12% of young people. (page 1)

⇨ Provided a vegetarian diet is well balanced, it should provide all of the nutrients needed by the body throughout life. (page 2)

⇨ Serious deficiencies of minerals are not widespread in vegetarian populations. (page 3)

⇨ In a survey conducted on behalf of The Vegetarian Society the majority of people said that they gave up meat and fish because they did not morally approve of killing animals, or because they objected to the ways in which animals are kept, treated and killed for food. (page 5)

⇨ People become vegetarian for three main reasons: health, taste or ethics. (page 8)

⇨ A study published in the International Journal of Obesity confirmed that vegetarians gain less weight than meat-eaters as they grow older. (page 9)

⇨ Intelligent children may be more likely to be vegetarian as adults, suggests a University of Southampton-led study published online by the British Medical Journal. (page 10)

⇨ Vegetarianism has been associated with a reduction in several of the established risk factors for coronary heart disease (CHD), including more favourable blood lipid profile, lower body mass index and lower blood pressure. (page 11)

⇨ Lean red meat contains a variety of different nutrients, including pro-tein, hearthealthy monounsaturates and omega3 fats, plus a wide variety of vitamins and minerals. (page 12)

⇨ Globally, meat consumption is increasing at a phenomenal rate. In the last 40 years, consumption has grown from 56 to 89 kilos of meat per person, per year in Europe and from 89 to 124 kilos in the US. Forty years ago, the Chinese were eating only 4 kilos of meat pp/pa – that figure has now reached 54 kilos and is still rising. (page 13)

⇨ Whilst in the UK and EU we have made great strides in phasing out some of the worst factory farming systems, globally, factory farming is increasing rapidly to meet the growing demand for meat. In the US, most meat is from highly intensive systems. (page 13)

⇨ A GfK NOP poll commissioned by the Vegetarian Society showed that, despite 95% of respondents saying they were not a vegetarian, only 13% agreed with the statement 'I don't really care what happens to farm animals'. (page 14)

⇨ Latest research from MINTEL shows that sales for meat such as venison, pheasant and grouse soared 46% between 2004 and 2006, to reach £57 million last year. (page 15)

⇨ Overall, Waitrose was found to be the most vegetarian and vegan friendly supermarket in Britain owing to its provision of meat-and dairy-free products across the spectrum. (page 20)

⇨ Meat is what dieticians call a 'complete' protein. Meat, fish, poultry, eggs, cheese and milk contain all of the eight essential amino acids needed by the body for growth and development. Soya and quinoa, a South American seed, are the only two vegetarian foods that contain a balance of all eight amino acids. (page 21)

⇨ In recent years, there has been an increase in the demand for free-range products by a public that is becoming more aware of both the health and moral implications of eating factory-farmed meat and eggs. (page 29)

⇨ 56 per cent of people in the UK would dump their usual supermarket in search of higher animal welfare products, says a new Eurobarometer survey. (page 31)

⇨ The Freedom Food mark seen on eggs, dairy, meat, poultry and salmon products means the animals involved have been reared, handled, transported and slaughtered to high standards devised and monitored by the RSPCA. (page 34)

⇨ Britain must continue to intensify its farming practices to meet soaring demand for cheap food and prevent shortages, a leading agricultural expert has said. (page 36)

⇨ Consumers bought some 2.04 billion free range, barn and organic eggs last year, up from just 1.64 billion in 2002 – an impressive 24% increase. Sales of free range eggs in particular have really started to boil over, rising some 31% since 2002 alone. (page 37)

⇨ Battery egg production in this country will be illegal by 2012, when a Europewide ban is due to come into force. (page 38)

GLOSSARY

Animal sentience
Animal sentience refers to animals' capability for being aware of sensations and emotions, of feeling pain and suffering, and of experiencing a state of wellbeing.

B12
B12 is a vitamin which helps red blood cells and bone marrow form in the body. It also helps maintain healthy cardiovascular and nervous systems. B12 only occurs naturally in animal products. However, vegans can ensure they get enough B12 by taking supplements or eating fortified foods.

Free-range
Meat and eggs labelled free-range have been produced on farms in which the animals are able to roam outdoors – in other words, they are not intensively reared in small cages. However, groups including PETA have claimed that the term free-range is misleading to consumers.

Fruitarian
A fruitarian excludes all foods of animal origin from their diet, as well as pulses and cereals.

Game
Wild animals which are hunted for food – for example, grouse, pheasant, venison and rabbit. Sales of game in the UK soared 46% between 2004 and 2006. It has been argued that eating game is healthier, more ethical and more sustainable than eating farmed meat.

Intensive farming
Also called battery farming. This refers to animals reared in large numbers in a small area, often in cages, for reasons of cost and efficiency.

Iron
Iron is a mineral used by the human body for carrying oxygen from lungs to tissues around the body. Much of the iron intake in an omnivorous diet comes from red meat – however, iron can also be found in pulses, green vegetables and fortified breakfast cereals. According to the British Medical Association, vegetarians are no more likely to suffer from anaemia than meat eaters.

Lacto-ovo-vegetarian
A lacto-ovo-vegetarian excludes all meat (including fish and poultry) from their diet, but still consumes dairy products and eggs. This is the most common type of vegetarian in the UK.

Lacto-vegetarian
A lacto-vegetarian excludes all meat (including fish and poultry) and eggs from their diet, but still consumes milk and milk products.

Macrobiotic
Sometimes referred to as 'Zen Macrobiotic'. The diet progresses through a series of levels, gradually eliminating all animal produce, fruit and vegetables and, at the highest level, leading to a restricted diet of cereal (brown rice) only. Fluids may also be severely restricted.

Omnivorous
The term omnivorous is applied to a diet containing a mixture of meat and plant-based foods. The equivalent term for a diet containing only meat and no vegetables is carnivorous, whereas a diet of only plant-based foods and no meat is called herbivorous. However, the terms herbivorous and carnivorous are usually only used with reference to the animal kingdom.

Pesco-vegetarian
Someone who excludes all red meat and poultry, but eats fish and other animal products, may sometimes be referred to as pesco-vegetarian. However, some 'full' vegetarians (those who exclude all meat) object to this label as misleading, believing that only those who eat no meat at all should refer to themselves as vegetarian.

Protein
Protein is essential for the growth and repair of tissues in the human body. It is made up of amino acids, some of which are known as 'essential amino acids' because the body can't make them itself. It's important to get some of each of these essential amino acids at the same time, but only animal products such as meat, eggs and dairy products contain the complete mix. Therefore, vegans need to make sure they combine the correct food types.

'Semi' or 'demi' vegetarian
Some people who exclude only red meat, or all meats except fish and other animal products, may refer to themselves as semi or demi vegetarians. However, some 'full' vegetarians (those who exclude all meat) object to this label as misleading.

Vegan
A vegan is a type of vegetarian who excludes not only meat and meat products from their diet, but also eggs, dairy products and honey (that is, they exclude any food deriving from an animal source).

Vegetarian
Most commonly, when someone is referred to as a vegetarian, it means that they do not eat meat, poultry, game or fish, and will also avoid slaughterhouse by-products such as gelatine, rennet and animal fats. Most vegetarians do eat dairy products and free-range eggs (lacto-ovo-vegetarian). In the last ten years, the number of vegetarians in the UK has more than doubled.

INDEX

Additional Resources

Other Issues *titles*
If you are interested in researching further some of the issues raised in *Vegetarian and Vegan Diets*, you may like to read the following titles in the **Issues** series:
⇨Vol. 88 Food and Nutrition (ISBN 978 1 86168 289 5)
⇨Vol. 103 Animal Rights (ISBN 978 1 86168 317 5)
⇨Vol. 123 Young People and Health (ISBN 978 1 86168 362 5)
For more information about these titles, visit our website at www.independence.co.uk/publicationslist

Useful organisations
You may find the websites of the following organisations useful for further research:

⇨RSPCA: www.rspca.org.uk

⇨The Vegetarian Society: www.vegsoc.org

⇨Compassion in World Farming: www.ciwf.org.uk

⇨People for the Ethical Treatment of Animals (PETA): www.peta.org.uk

ACKNOWLEDGEMENTS

The publisher is grateful for permission to reproduce the following material.

While every care has been taken to trace and acknowledge copyright, the publisher tenders its apology for any accidental infringement or where copyright has proved untraceable. The publisher would be pleased to come to a suitable arrangement in any such case with the rightful owner.

Chapter One: Vegetarians and Vegans

Vegetarianism, © TheSite.org, *Vegetarian and vegan diets*, © British Nutrition Foundation, *Going vegetarian*, © Vegetarian Society, *Vegetarian and vegan*, © Crown copyright is reproduced with the permission of Her Majesty's Stationery Office, *What makes a vegetarian?*, © Nestlé, *Vegetarians can cut cancer risk*, © Vegetarian Society, *Questions to think about*, © British Humanist Association, *Vegetarianism and IQ*, © University of Southampton, *Vegetarian nutrition*, © British Nutrition Foundation, *Red meat*, © Meat and Livestock Commission, *Eat less meat – it's costing the earth*, © Compassion in World Farming, *Meat eaters care but carry on regardless…*, © Vegetarian Society, *Brits go wild for game*, © Mintel, *Happy hunting*, © Guardian Newspapers Ltd, *We should eat horse meat, says Ramsay*, © Telegraph Group Ltd, *Beastly ingredients – to avoid!* © Animal Aid, *Vegetarian-friendly supermarkets*, © Animal Aid, *Scientists measure red meat cancer risks*, © Cancer Research UK, *Red meat linked to breast cancer*, © University of Leeds, *Let's meat up again*, © Telegraph Group Ltd, *Why eat meat?* © Telegraph Group Ltd, *Going dairy-free*, © Animal Aid, *Veganism and the issue of protein*, © PETA, *Being vegan – a guide*, © Vegan Society.

Chapter Two: Animal Welfare

Animal sentience, © Compassion in World Farming, *Free-range eggs and meat: conning consumers?*, © PETA, *Ethical shoppers*, © Compassion in World Farming, *A humanist discussion of animal welfare*, © British Humanist Association, *Eat for animal welfare*, © TheSite.org, *Freedom food*, © RSPCA, *Animal welfare on organic farms*, © Soil Association, *'Only intensive farming' will feed Britain*, © Guardian Newspapers Ltd, *Sunny side up for sales of ethically-positioned eggs*, © Mintel, *The price of eggs*, © Guardian Newspapers Ltd.

Illustrations

Pages 1, 22, 32: Angelo Madrid; pages 4, 25: Bev Aisbett; pages 13, 28, 37: Simon Kneebone; pages 15, 30, 34, 38: Don Hatcher.

Photographs

Page 3: Patrycja Cieszkowska-Krystosik; page 12: Marcela Lopez; page 17: Louise Clarke; page 19: Luis Cesar Tejo; page 29: Ove Tøpfer; page 36: Corné van Braak.

And with thanks to the team: Mary Chapman, Sophie Crewsdon, Sandra Dennis and Jan Haskell.

Lisa Firth and Cobi Smith
Cambridge
September, 2007